Karl Jaspers

Kurt Salamun

Karl Jaspers

Physician, Psychologist, Philosopher,
Political Thinker

palgrave
macmillan

Kurt Salamun
Graz, Austria

ISBN 978-3-476-05895-9   ISBN 978-3-476-05896-6   (eBook)
https://doi.org/10.1007/978-3-476-05896-6

This Palgrave Macmillan imprint is published by the registered company Springer-Verlag GmbH, DE, part of Springer Nature.
The registered company address is: Heidelberger Platz 3, 14197 Berlin, Germany

Preface

The 50th anniversary of the death of Karl Jaspers (1883–1969) is a special occasion to attempt a retrospective look at the perilous and difficult course of his life, the diverse body of his work, and the impact he has had to date. Currently, interest in Jaspers' philosophy is on the rise. He is increasingly perceived as an important philosopher, humanist and moralist of the twentieth century, and his work is more and more frequently questioned as to how far thought-provoking impulses and impulses for action can be gained from it for the present. Standing in the liberal-enlightenment European tradition of Immanuel Kant and Max Weber, Jaspers is a European humanist whose openness to foreign, non-European cultures (China, India) can serve as a model.

This book first informs about the personality of Jaspers, his incurable illness, happy marriage, life under the Naz-iregime, about his activities as a psychiatrist, researcher, academic teacher, existential philosopher and political writer.

Then follows an introduction to Jaspers' thoughts on the meaning of life in borderline situations and interpersonal communication, on the question of God and the meaning of history, the defense of the idea of democracy, as well as on his concept of a world history of philosophy. Also relevant again today are Jaspers' critique of narrow nationalistic and authoritarian-totalitarian ways of thinking in politics, as well as his warning against the possibility of nuclear war. In all these areas, a liberal ethos of humanity reveals itself, which forms the moral background of his thinking.

The genesis of this book can be traced back to my decades-long preoccupation with Jaspers. One impulse for this was also my wife's constant interest in this thinker; I owe her much advice on content and style.

I also received valuable stimuli from lectures and discussions with important Jaspers interpreters, especially with Jaspers' last personal assistant Hans Saner, with Jeanne Hersch, Reiner Wiehl, Alan M. Olson, Gregory J. Walters, Giorgio Penzo, Czeslawa Piecuch, Andreas Cesana, Anton Hügli, Dominic Kaegi, Oliver Immel, Bernd Weidmann and others whom I cannot mention by name here.

I dedicate this book to my friend Hans Saner, who passed away on Boxing Day 2017, and whose creative insights into Jaspers' personality and work will often accompany me in communicative reflections.

Editorial notes: Works by Jaspers are abbreviated in the text by sigles (cf. list of sigles). References to correspondence and other Jaspers writings can be found in the bibliography. In the text, the "ß" spelling has been changed to "ss". Book titles are highlighted in small caps, names only in italics.

Graz, Austria   Kurt Salamun
15 January 2019

List of Sigles (Letters Concern the German Editions)

AP	Allgemeine Psychopathologie. Ein Leitfaden für Studierende, Ärzte und Psychologen [1913]. 9th ed. Berlin, Heidelberg 1973. (General Psychopathology. A guide for students, physicians and psychologists).
Ant	Antwort. Zur Kritik meiner Schrift "Wohin treibt die Bundesrepublik?" München 1967. (Response. On the criticism of my paper "Wohin treibt die Bundesrepublik?")
Aut	Philosophische Autobiographie. Erweiterte Neuausgabe München 1977. (Philosophical autobiography. Expanded new edition).
AZ	Der Arzt im technischen Zeitalter. Technik und Medizin, Arzt und Patient, Kritik der Psychotherapie. München 1986 (The doctor in the technical age. Technology and medicine, doctor and patient, critique of psychotherapy).
AZM	Die Atombombe und die Zukunft des Menschen. Politisches Bewusstsein in unserer Zeit. [1958]. 6. Aufl. München, Zürich 1982 (The atomic bomb and the future of man. Political consciousness in our time. 6th ed. Munich, Zurich 1982).
BR	Wohin treibt die Bundesrepublik? Tatsachen-Gefahren-Chancen. München 1966. Neuausgabe 1988. (Where is the Federal Republic drifting? Facts - Dangers - Chances. Munich 1966, new edition 1988).
Ch	Chiffren der Transzendenz. München 1970. Neuausgabe unter dem Titel "Die Chiffren der Transzendenz" mit zwei Vorworten von Anton Hügli und Hans Saner. Basel 2011. (Ciphers of transcendence. [1970]. New edition under the title "Die Chiffern der Transzendenz" with two epilogues by Anton Hügli and Hans Saner, Basel 2011).
E	Existenzphilosophie. Drei Vorlesungen. Berlin/Leipzig 1938. 4. Aufl. Berlin/New York 1974. (Existential Philosophy. Three lectures). New edition with an introductory and passage commentary. Edited by Dominic Kaegi. In: Karl Jaspers Schriften zur Existenzphilosophie. In: Karl Jaspers Gesamtausgabe, I/8, Basel 2018, 99–160.
Einf	Einführung in die Philosophie. Zwölf Radiovorträge. Zürich 1950. 23. Aufl. München, Zürich 1983. (Introduction to Philosophy. Twelve radio lectures)
Ent	Karl Jaspers/Rudolf Bultmann, Die Frage der Entmythologisierung. [1954]. Neuauflage mit einer Einführung von Heinrich Ott. München 1981. (The Question of Demythologization, by Karl Jaspers and Rudolf Bultmann New edition with an introduction by Heinrich Ott. Munich 1981).
FW	Freiheit und Wiedervereinigung. Über Aufgaben deutscher Politik [1960].Neuausgabe mit einem Vorwort von Willy Brandt. München, Zürich 1990. (Freedom and Reunification. On the tasks of German politics. [1960]. New edition with a foreword by Willy Brandt. Munich, Zurich 1990).
Gl	Der philosophische Glaube. Gastvorlesungen [1948]. 8. Aufl. Zürich, München 1985. (The philosophical faith. Guest Lectures. [1948]. 8th ed. Zurich, Munich 1985).
GP	Die großen Philosophen. Erster Band. München 1959. (The great philosophers. Volume 1. Munich 1959).

GSZ	Die geistige Situation der Zeit. [1931]. 5. Aufl. Berlin 1971. (The spiritual situation of the times. 5th ed. Berlin 1971).
HV	Heimweh und Verbrechen. [1909]. In: Karl Jaspers, Gesammelte Schriften zur Psychopathologie. Berlin, Heidelberg, New York 1953, 1–84. (Homesick and Crime. dissertation 1909).
HS	Hoffnung und Sorge. Schriften zur deutschen Politik 1945–1965. München 1965. (Hope and Concern. Writings about German policy 1945–1965).
IU	Die Idee der Universität. [1923, Neufassung 1946 sowie 1961 mit Kurt Rossmann]; Neuausgabe und kommentiert von Oliver Immel 2016. In: Karl Jaspers Gesamtausgabe: Schriften zur Universitätsidee, I/21, Basel 2016. 255–443 (The Idea of the University. [1923, new edition 1946, and 1961 with Kurt Rossmann], new edition of 1961 with an introductory and passage commentary edited by Oliver Immel. In: Karl Jaspers Collected Works, I/21, Basel 2016. 255–443).
KlSch	Kleine Schule des philosophischen Denkens. München 1965. Neuausgabe 1974 (Little school of philosophical thought. New edition Munich 1974).
MW	Max Weber. Gesammelte Schriften. Mit einer Einführung von Dieter Henrich. München, Zürich 1988. (Max Weber. Collected Writings. With an introduction by Dieter Henrich. Munich, Zurich 1988).
N	Nietzsche. Einführung in das Verständnis seines Philosophierens. [1935]. 4. Aufl. Berlin, New York 1981. (Nietzsche. Introduction to the understanding of his philosophizing. [1935]. 4th ed. Berlin, New York 1981).
NH	Notizen zu Martin Heidegger. Hg. Von Hans Saner. München 1978. (Notes on Martin Heidegger. Ed. by Hans Saner. Munich 1978).
NPL	Nachlaß zur Philosophischen Logik. Edited by Hans Saner and Marc Hänggi. München 1991.
PG	Der philosophische Glaube. Gastvorlesungen [1948]. 7. Aufl. München 1981. (The philosophical faith. Guest Lectures. [1948]. 7th ed. Munich 1981).
PGO	Der philosophische Glaube angesichts der Offenbarung.[1962]. Neuausgabe mit einem Kommentar hg. von Bernd Weidmann. In: Karl Jaspers Gesamtausgabe, I/13, Basel 2016. (Philosophical faith and revelation. [1962]. New edition with an introductory and passage commentary. Ed. Bernd Weidmann. In: Karl Jaspers Collected Works I/13,95–517).
PhI-III	Philosophie. 3 Bd. Bd. I: Philosophische Weltorientierung. Bd. II: Existenzerhellung. Bd. III: Metaphysik. [1932]. 4. Aufl. Berlin, Heidelberg, New York 1973. (Philosophy. 3 vols. Vol. I: Philosophical world orientation. Vol. II: Existential Elucidation. Vol. III: Metaphysics. [1932]. 4th ed. Berlin, Heidelberg, New York 1973).
Prov	Provokationen – Gespräche und Interviews. Hg. Von Hans Saner. München 1969. (Provocations—Conversations and Interviews. Edited by Hans Saner. Munich 1969).
PW	Psychologie der Weltanschauungen. [1919]. 6. Aufl. Berlin, Heidelberg, New York 1971. Neuauflage München 1985. (Psychology of worldviews. [1919]. 6th ed. Berlin, Heidelberg, New York 1971. New edition. Munich 1985).
RA	Rechenschaft und Ausblick. Reden und Aufsätze. [1951]. 2. Aufl. München 1958. (Accountability and outlook. Speeches and essays. [1951]. 2nd ed. Munich 1958).
Sch	Die Schuldfrage. [1946]. Neuauflage München 1987. (The question of guilt. [1946]. New edition Munich 1987).
SchW	Schicksal und Wille. Autobiographische Schriften. Hg. Von Hans Saner. München 1967. (Fate and Will. Autobiographical writings. Ed. by Hans Saner. Munich 1967).
UZG	Vom Ursprung und Ziel der Geschichte. [1949]. Neuausgabe mit Kommentar hg. von Kurt Salamun. In: Karl Jaspers Gesamtausgabe, I/10, Basel 2017. (The origin and goal of history. [1949]. New edition with an introductory and passage commentary, ed. by Kurt Salamun. In: Karl Jaspers Collected Works I/10, Basel 2017).

VE	Vernunft und Existenz. Fünf Vorlesungen [1935]. 3. Aufl. München 1984. Neuausgabe mit Einleitung und Stellenkommentar hg. von Dominic Kaegi. In: Karl Jaspers Schriften zur Existenzphilosophie. In: Karl Jaspers Gesamtausgabe, I/8, Basel 2018, 3–98. (Reason and Existence. Five lectures. [1935]. 3rd ed. Munich 1984. New edition with an introductory and passage commentary, ed. by Dominic Kaegi. In: Karl Jaspers Collected Works I/8, Basel 2018, 3–98).
VWZ	Vernunft und Widervernunft in unserer Zeit. Drei Gastvorlesungen. München 1950. (Reason and Counter-Reason in Our Time. Three guest lectures. Munich 1950).
W	Von der Wahrheit. Philosophische Logik. Erster Band. (1947). 3. Aufl. München 1983. (Of Truth. Philosophical Logic. Vol. 1. (1947). 3rd ed. Munich 1983).
WGP	Weltgeschichte der Philosophie. Einleitung. Aus dem Nachlass Hg. Von Hans Saner. München, Zürich 1982. (World history of philosophy. Introduction. From the estate. Ed. by Hans Saner. Munich, Zurich 1982).

Contents

Stages of an Arduous but Happy Life

1

1.1 Early Imprints in the Parental Home, Childhood and Adolescence

Karl (Theodor) Jaspers was born in Oldenburg on 23 February 1883. The father was a lawyer, bank director, former district governor and member of the Oldenburg state parliament. The mother Henriette, née Tantzen, came from a wealthy farming family from Butjadingen near the North Sea coast. In his autobiographical writings, Jaspers repeatedly emphasizes how strongly his parental home influenced his basic ideological attitude. Thus, he once characterizes the political sentiments of his immediate ancestors as a "conservative-liberal, oppositional attitude, tending toward democracy through aristocracy." (Aut 123) About the education he and his two siblings (Enno and Erna) received, he states that it was based on a worldview that was characterized by a "claim of unrestricted truthfulness" but also "by an ignoring of the Christian, without polemics" (cf. SchW 84).

In reminiscences of his school days, he reports that he initially suffered from school anxiety when he first started school.

> My resistance to school could not have helped. When things got serious, at first the way to school every day was a torture. I was escorted there for weeks because I was too frightened on my own, especially to protect me from strange dogs who were so barbaric and did not have the calmness of our hunting dog, and from the policemen who seemed so dangerous to me, until once there was a friendly conversation with one of them. (SchW 57)

Jaspers, as a high school student, seems to have been constantly plagued by fears of school failure.

> All these years I was worried about coming along; out of this worry I was diligent. For my memory was not good, I memorized the spelling very laboriously and late, I forgot as vocabulary quickly, languages were difficult for me. In the upper classes I became a better pupil. But, although I was then mostly the third of about twenty pupils according to class rank, I was always afraid of being left behind. (SchW 61)

© Springer-Verlag GmbH Germany, part of Springer Nature 2022
K. Salamun, *Karl Jaspers*, https://doi.org/10.1007/978-3-476-05896-6_1

Despite or precisely because of these fears of failure, Jaspers developed a high degree of self-confidence and independence as a grammar school student. This is evidenced by behavioral patterns from everyday school life at the humanistic grammar school he attended in Oldenburg: for example, standing up to the pressure to conform to which he was subjected by refusing to join any of the three student fraternities established at the school; or demonstrative resistance to disciplinary measures that seemed pointless to him and that the militaristic-authoritarian headmaster wanted to impose on him (cf. SchW 18–20).

In his PHILOSOPHISCHE AUTOBIOGRAPHIE (henceforth: AUTOBIOGRAPHIE) Jaspers writes about it retrospectively:

> Taught by my father, I advocated the principle that there was a difference between the order of teaching and the military discipline that unjustly invaded the school. That was the spirit of opposition, the headmaster solemnly explained to me one day. It was peculiar to my family and must be rejected by him. (Aut 9)

At graduation, Jaspers' aversion to the school's principal, who was also the Latin teacher, became apparent once again when the latter offered Jaspers to give the speech at the graduation ceremony in Latin and Jaspers gave the provocative response:

> No, I do not want this … because we have not learned so much Latin that we can speak Latin; this artificially prepared speech is a deception of the audience. (SchW 68–69)

As a formative childhood memory, Jaspers mentions the deep impression that experiences of the sea and the tides at the North Sea made on him.

> I grew up with the sea. [...] Even as a child, I experienced infinity unreflectively at the sea. Since then, the sea has been to me like the self-evident background of life in general. The sea is the vivid presence of the infinite. The waves are infinite. Everything is always in motion, nowhere the fixed and the whole in the nevertheless palpable infinite order. Seeing the sea became for me the most glorious thing there is in nature. (SchW 15)

One consequence of Jaspers' enthusiasm for the sea and nature was the decision to work at the zoological station on Helgoland during two semester breaks (of the years 1904 and 1905). He conducted nature studies there (collecting and categorizing stones, preparing small animals, etc.).

When Jaspers undertook a trip to Italy in the spring of 1902, he reported enthusiastically in letters to his parents about fascinating experiences with the Mediterranean flora. But architectural buildings and works of art from the early and high Renaissance – the latter he admired in the museums of Florence and Rome – also left a deep impression.[1] From early childhood he was able to observe his father drawing and painting, so he developed an early interest in the fine arts.

---

[1] Cf. Suzanne Kirkbright (ed.), *Karl Jaspers Italienbriefe 1902*, Heidelberg 2006, 76, 80, 94.

1.2   Serious Cuts in the Life Course

1.2.1   The Incurable Disease

At the age of eighteen, Jaspers had to take note of a diagnosis about his state of health that explained repeated bouts of weakness and exhaustion. The diagnosis was: incurable lung disease and heart failure. Research reports by capacities in medicine at the time gave patients with this disease a very short life expectancy. Jaspers reports:

> I read a treatise by Rudolf Virchow, which described my illness in detail and made the prognosis: at the latest in the thirties of their lives these sick people perish from general suppuration. (Aut 12–13)

The lung disease, known in medical terminology as "bronchiectasis", results from a congenital lack of elasticity of the bronchial tubes, which leads to a constant build-up of purulent secretions in the lungs, resulting in a chronic cough and the risk of pneumonia.

To counter this danger, Jaspers himself developed the following method of treatment: he coughed out the secretions from his lungs several times a day, lying on a divan in various lateral positions of the body. This procedure, together with the greatest possible physical rest and the avoidance of situations where there was a danger of viral infection, contributed to his reaching *the age of 86,* despite the constant impairment caused by the incurable disease.

In 1938 Jaspers put down on paper a detailed account of the nature, circumstances and consequences of the illness. He published this paper in 1968 under the title "Krankengeschichte" (history of illness) in the autobiographical writing SCHICKSAL UND WILLE (FATE AND WILL). In the AUTOBIOGRAPHIE, he describes how he experienced and coped with the illness situation in a detached self-analysis and without pathos, but nonetheless poignantly:

> All the decisions of my life were conditioned by a basic fact of my existence. From childhood I was organically ill (bronchiectasis and secondary heart failure) … The illness was not allowed to become the purpose of life by worrying about it. The task was to treat her properly, almost without consciousness, and to work as if she were not there. Everything had to be directed according to her without falling prey to her. Again and again I made mistakes. The necessities that followed from the illness intervened in every hour and in all plans … The consequence of the illness was an inner attitude that determined the way of working. Life had to be concentrated with the constant interruptions in order to be lived meaningfully at all. I was dependent on a relaxed way of studying, on grasping the essential, on the suddenness of the idea and the speed of the design. The chance lay in the tenacity to seize every good moment and to continue the work at all hazards. (Aut 12–13)

The fact that Jaspers accepted very few invitations to lecture during his academic career and avoided attending scientific congresses can be explained by his illness.

> Another consequence of the illness was that I could appear in public only under carefully observed conditions, and always briefly. Only in important exceptional cases did I undertake

journeys to give lectures and to take part in public discussions, always at the price of disturbing what I considered to be my normal state of health. (Aut 14)

Another note on the heavy burden of illness is found in a draft letter to *Martin Heidegger* from 1936:

To tell a little about myself: Physically, I live on the edge; the smallest demands – even travel – knock my body over. At the moment I am well able. Last year from July to October and in the weeks after until Christmas I was ill, had chills, bleeding – but everything is getting better.[2]

The complicated conditions under which Jaspers was once able to accept an invitation to give three consecutive lectures at the "Freies Deutsches Hochstift" in Frankfurt a. M. can be seen in his correspondence with *Ernst Beutler,* the long-time director and head of the Goethe-Haus in Frankfurt. The letter with which Jaspers accepted the invitation states, among other things:

And finally, something technical: because of a heart condition that has long prohibited me from standing, I give my lectures sitting down. Is it possible for me to sit behind the lectern for these lectures as well and take in the situation the day before? Also, can I be in a room on the same floor as the lecture hall in the fifteen minutes before the lecture? How high do you think the stairs are?[3]

In a letter dated 14 May 1946 to the Rector *Karl Heinrich Bauer,* who was the first Rector of Heidelberg University after the Second World War and with whom Jaspers worked closely in the organizational reconstruction of the university, he apologized for not attending a meeting with the following words:

Magnificence!
I apologize for my absence from today's Senate meeting. The reason is that I had a somewhat violent bronchial hemorrhage for three days. Sunday it got better, yesterday the secretion was free of blood, so that the lecture could be dared. However, I suppose I still have to be extra careful these days, as the secretion abnormality I have to put up with after every session longer than an hour would not be harmless now. Therefore, I ask for your kind medical understanding.[4]

There is an account of Jaspers' extraordinary handling of the illness by a doctor who provided him with medical care in Basel during the last six years of his life. There it is emphasized that Jaspers not only registered the manifestations of the disease precisely. As a medical doctor interested in natural science, he always tried to gain clarity about the processes in his body. He always wanted therapy proposals to be carefully justified.

---

[2] Martin Heidegger/Karl Jaspers, *Briefwechsel 1920–1963,* Frankfurt, München, Zürich 1990, 266.
[3] Karl Jaspers, Ernst Beutler, *Briefwechsel 1937–1960.* In: Dominic Kaegi, Reiner Wiehl (eds.), *Karl Jaspers Korrespondenzen, vol. 2 Philosophie,* Göttingen 2013, 95.
[4] Karl Jaspers, Karl Heinrich Bauer, *Briefwechsel 1945–1968,* Heidelberg 1983, 41.

Jaspers not only suffered the illness, but it was always also the object of scientific observation for him. In relation to it, he was both the suffering subject and the object of observation. As a rational patient he actively participated in the recognition and treatment of the undesirable natural process of the disease. His observations were the basis and supplement of my knowledge and conclusions. We made our knowledge available to each other in order to use it jointly in the therapeutic procedure.[5]

There is much to suggest that the constant, extreme danger to health has had an influence on key concepts of Jaspers' existential philosophy. In the thesis of the borderline situations of human life one can read an echo of this endangerment. For Jaspers, the struggle character of life represented a borderline situation of being human. Life often only gained a real meaning in the face of the principle limit of death. Jaspers himself had to fight illness daily and was often aware of the possibility of imminent death.

1.2.2   The Unconditionality and Happiness of the Marital Relationship

The meeting with his later wife, a sister of fellow student and friend *Ernst Mayer,* had a profound effect on Jaspers' life and philosophizing. He writes about their first meeting:

Loneliness, melancholy, self-confidence, everything changed when I met Gertrud Mayer at the age of 24, in 1907. Unforgettable for me was the moment when I entered her room for the first time with her brother ... It was as if it were a matter of course that the conversation soon turned to great fundamental questions of life, as if we had known each other for a long time. From the first hour there was an incomprehensible harmony between us, never expected to be possible. (Aut 15)

Gertrud Mayer came from a Jewish family with many children and had eight siblings. She had worked as a nurse in mental hospitals and was four years older than Jaspers. Of her siblings, the eldest brother, *Gustav Mayer,* became known as a social historian and researcher of the history of the labor movement. Another brother, *Ernst Mayer,* a fellow student and physician, repeatedly played an important role in Jaspers' life. In the AUTOBIOGRAPHIE, he acknowledges him as a close and imaginative collaborator on the main work of existential philosophy, the three vol. book PHILOSOPHIE (PHILOSOPHY).

Ernst has had the greatest significance for my philosophizing, both through his existence and through what he said. But he took a direct part in the elaboration of my three-volume "Philosophy". Without him this work would not have become what it is ... He was unique in devoted selflessness in which he treated my cause entirely as his own. He not only read all the manuscripts, but added critical notes to them. He had a hand in the structure of the chapters, in the factual and in the stylistic. He brought me not only the powerful impulse of his participation and demanding, but enrichments, improvements in great numbers. (Aut 50–51)

---

[5]Adolf Bernstein, Erinnerungen an Karl Jaspers. In: Klaus Piper, Hans Saner (eds.), *Erinnerungen an Karl Jaspers,* München, Zürich 1974, 290.

The closeness of *Ernst Mayer's* intellectual ties with Jaspers is documented in his own book DIALEKTIK DES NICHTWISSENS (DIALECTIC OF NON-KNOWING).[6] It contains in many parts some of the most insightful and immanent interpretations of Jaspers' existential-philosophical and metaphysical thinking of the time.

Jaspers and *Gertrud Mayer* married in 1910 and had a particularly happy marriage. Gertrud identified herself with Jaspers' work without reservation and supported him admirably. A friend of the couple reports:

> After her marriage, Mrs. Jaspers abandoned her own plans of study ... Thus she became her husband's first collaborator, and her merit cannot be overestimated. She copied all her husband's manuscripts over and over again. For no work has a final shape at once. She also helped by making critical comments, sharing with her husband the thoughts that came to her as she wrote. In addition, she read books for him and noted important passages.[7]

Klaus Piper, in whose publishing house numerous works by Jaspers have appeared and who experienced the Jaspers couple on many visits, wrote about this:

> This marriage showed itself to the friendly visitor as something unique in the mixture of cordial connection with some small, affectionately critical signals from one to the other. The common ground in philosophizing was the natural medium in which both lived. This was not, however, a life in a world-segregated ivory tower. The problematic, the dangerous or the comical in the human environment was thoroughly discussed, considered with participation and concern. Wordless help was given.[8]

The wordless help alluded to here included, for example, financial assistance to needy students who, returning from deployment at the front after the end of the Second World War, approached the Jaspers couple. In particular, one must mention the financial support for Jaspers' brother-in-law *Ernst Mayer*. He lost his medical practice in Berlin during the Nazi regime and had to emigrate with his family to Holland, where he lived penniless in hiding. After the war, he was not allowed to practice medicine there because he had not obtained his license to practice medicine in Holland. That the resulting *thriftiness* of Jaspers and his wife should not be interpreted as the result of "greed for money" is well understood. This unjust judgement was made in the memoirs of his youth by *Golo Mann*, a son of the Nobel Prize winner *Thomas Mann*.[9] *Golo Mann* had received his doctorate from Jaspers in Heidelberg in 1930 with a thesis entitled "Zum Begriff des Einzelnen, des Ich und des Individuellen bei Hegel". He visited the couple frequently and seems to have competed for the attention and affection that Jaspers gave *Hannah Arendt*. *Arendt* was also a doctoral student of Jaspers and a frequent visitor to the couple.

---

[6] Basel 1950.

[7] Wilhelmine Drescher, *Erinnerungen an Karl Jaspers in Heidelberg*, Meisenheim am Glan 1975, 22.

[8] Klaus Piper, Karl Jaspers, Erinnerungen aus verlegerischer Zusammenarbeit. In: Klaus Piper, Hans Saner (eds.), *Erinnerungen an Karl Jaspers*, 193.

[9] Cf. Golo Mann, *Erinnerungen und Gedanken. Eine Jugend in Deutschland*, Frankfurt a. M. 1986, 318.

It stands to reason that the deep emotional and spiritual relationship with his wife influenced Jaspers' philosophizing about interpersonal communication. *Hans Saner*, Jaspers' assistant in Basel and editor of many of his writings, assesses the influence of this relationship on Jaspers' thinking as follows:

> What is said about communication and love, perhaps the whole second volume of *Philosophie*, would have remained unsaid in this depth without the bond with his life companion.[10]

Jaspers also confirms this in AUTOBIOGRAPHIE when he states there:

> Only with my wife did I come to the path of loving struggle, the path of life-perpetuating, never-finished, unreserved, therefore inexhaustible communication. (Aut 124)

That the harmonious and loving relationship with his parents may have played a role in Jaspers' understanding of personal communication is suggested by *Suzanne Kirkbright* in her JASPERS-BIOGRAPHIE (JASPERS BIOGRAPHY), in which she has reviewed the correspondence between Jaspers and his family members.[11]

1.3   Period of Study, Dissertation and Academic Career

After graduating from high school (1901), Jaspers began studying law in Freiburg (1901), Heidelberg (1901/1902), and Munich (1902). In Freiburg, there were several attempts to recruit him for a student fraternity, but he firmly rejected such offers. Looking back, he describes the negative attitude towards student fraternities at that time:

> Hateful to me were all corporations, whether fraternities or corps. They appeared to me as the enemy of independence, as a method of levelling people, as a crawling under of those who do not have the strength for solitude, – but above all as the realization of absurd manners, of an unfounded self-confidence through wearing colours, of a pomposity with things that did not seem important to me, in addition as a barbarism as it is exercised in the regular pubs. (Jaspers, Diary Studies 1901–1907, 1 (1996), 12)

After three semesters of study, in which he was less concerned with jurisprudence than with art history and philosophy, he changed to the study of medicine. This decision was obviously partly conditioned by the illness.

Jaspers first studied in Berlin in the winter semester of 1902, where he completed the natural sciences, then went to Göttingen for the clinical subjects in 1904 and to Heidelberg in 1906. At the beginning of 1909 he completed his medical studies there with the state examination. In an autobiographical writing, which he compiled in 1938 with recourse to earlier diary entries, he describes events and impressions

---

[10] Cf. Hans Saner, *Preface* to Karl Jaspers, *Schicksal und Wille*, München 1967, 13.
[11] Cf. Suzanne Kirkbright, *Karl Jaspers. A Biography. Navigation in Truth*, New Haven, London 2005.

from his student days. In addition to harsh judgments of some professors, there are also self-reflections on his shyness about communication at the time and on methodological aspects of studying the large amount of material that he had to acquire in the natural sciences and anatomy during his medical studies.

> My work was intense, but then lasted only a short time each time. A lot of rest time and then quick access. Mere stubborn diligence has always seemed to me to be spiritual laziness … One must not be passively led by the pages of the book, the schemes of practicals and teachers. Spiritual failure is when one inhibits darkly emerging germs within oneself in favor of the obediently followed path. It is indolent to abandon oneself to the order of books and curricula. […] There is a spirit in us that is anticipatory of the whole, which then illuminates itself step by step. (Jaspers, Diary Studies 1901–1907, 2 (1997), 44)

Jaspers finished his studies with the dissertation HEIMWEH UND VERBRECHEN (HOMESICKNESS AND CRIME). The work belongs to the field of forensic psychiatry. He describes the topic in the following introductory sentences:

> For a long time, the crimes (murder and arson) committed with unbelievable cruelty and ruthless brutality by delicate creatures, young and good-natured girls still in their infancy, have aroused interest. The contradiction between the deed and the perpetrator, the lack of motive or insufficient motivation, and therefore the mysterious and incomprehensible nature of the events aroused sympathy or disgust. (HV 1)

The fact that young girls who came from humble backgrounds and went into "service" with wealthy families as child caretakers committed murders of the children entrusted to them and arsons against the houses of their employers is something Jaspers systematically tries to explain in terms of a specific form of homesickness that can be traced back to social degradation and isolation.

1.4   From Psychiatry Via Psychology to Existential Philosophy

After completing his medical studies, Jaspers worked for seven years as a scientific volunteer assistant (i.e. assistant without salary) at the Neurological Department of Internal Medicine at the Psychiatric University Clinic in Heidelberg. The head of this clinic, *Franz Nissl*, an eminent brain histologist, had taken a liking to Jaspers' dissertation. The constructive-critical climate of discussion that prevailed among the physicians and researchers at the Heidelberg Psychiatric Clinic at that time was something Jaspers repeatedly emphasized with gratitude in later memoirs. He worked intensively scientifically in this climate for six years.

During this time, he wrote a variety of book announcements and book reviews published in various journals: *Zeitschrift für die gesamte Neurologie und Psychiatrie, Zeitschrift für angewandte Psychologie, Zeitschrift für Psychotherapie und medizinische Psychologie, Archiv für die gesamte Psychologie, Jahrbuch für psychoanalytische und psychopathologische Forschung, Jahrbuch für Psychologie und Physiologie der Sinnesorgane.*

In addition, he published articles on the topics: Jealousy Delusions. A Contribution to the Question: 'Development of a Personality' or 'Process'? (1910), The methods of intelligence testing and the concept of dementia (1910), On the analysis of delusions (1911), The phenomenological direction of research in psychopathology (1912), Causal and 'intelligible' connections between fate and psychosis in dementia praecox (schizophrenia) (1913).

The culmination of his research work as a psychopathologist was the publication of the book ALLGEMEINE PSYCHOPATHOLOGIE (GENERAL PSYCHOPATHOLOGY) (1913). This book made Jaspers so well known that during the First World War he was offered the succession to *Nissl* to the chair of psychiatry by the dean of the medical faculty in Heidelberg. However, Jaspers had to decline in consideration of his chronic illness. As a response to this book, he received honorary memberships from psychiatric societies all over the world until his old age.

One would be misjudging Jaspers' activity at the Heidelberg Psychiatric Clinic if one thought that he worked there only as a theorist and methodologist. This misconception is corrected by *Wolfram Schmitt,* who was employed at this clinic for some time:

> Jaspers' activity at the clinic, however, was not exhausted in scientific work and discussion, but he also participated, albeit to a lesser extent than his colleagues, in the therapeutic practice of the clinic. Thus, in the atmosphere of the clinic, he developed not only into a theoretically oriented researcher, but also into a psychiatrist with practical experience. He was present at the clinical rounds, treated selected patients, participated in the psychiatric care of the students, once also took over the psychiatric outpatient clinic on a deputy basis and repeatedly acted as a judicial expert. A number of forensic reports and medical records, which are still preserved in the Heidelberg Psychiatric Clinic, bear witness to his psychiatric experience.[12]

The special merits of ALLGEMEINE PSYCHOPATHOLOGIE lie in methodological insights and efforts at clarification, through which Jaspers wanted to pave the way for the development of psychiatry into a methodologically independent scientific discipline. He made it his task to elaborate a systematics of the previous research approaches, whereby he was primarily concerned with making clear the scope and limits of the methods used in these research approaches.

In 1913 he habilitated with the ALLGEMEINE PSYCHOPATHOLOGIE not at the Medical Faculty, but at the Philosophical Faculty of the University of Heidelberg for the subject Psychology. In 1916 he became Extra-ordinarius for psychology, but the attempt to get a psychology institute approved failed. In 1919, one of the psychological lectures was published under the title PSYCHOLOGIE DER WELTANSCHAUUNGEN (PSYCHOLOGY OF WORLDVIEWS). In this book, under the influence of *Max Weber's* methodological conception of ideal types, a typology of attitudes and worldviews is sketched. Under the label of an understanding psychology, important themes of Jaspers' later existential philosophy are already anticipated.

---

[12] Wolfram Schmitt, Karl Jaspers als Psychiater und sein Einfluss auf die Psychiatrie. In: Joachim Leonhard (ed.), *Karl Jaspers in seiner Heidelberger Zeit,* Heidelberg 1983, 23.

On the basis of this book, Jaspers was appointed Extra-ordinarius in Heidelberg in 1920, and Ordinarius of Philosophy in 1921. Previously, he had turned down two appointments to chairs of philosophy in Greifswald and Kiel. In the years that followed, he had to fight out a controversy in Heidelberg with a renowned colleague, namely the New Kantian *Heinrich Rickert*. *Rickert* did not want to respect Jaspers as a colleague in philosophy because he had no background in philosophy but came from medicine and psychology.

In 1931 Jaspers published the small book DIE GEISTIGE SITUATION DER ZEIT (THE SPIRITUAL SITUATION OF THE TIME), which was widely distributed as the thousandth volume of the "Sammlung Göschen". In it, levelling and massification tendencies are a main theme, to which individuals in the modern age are exposed under the influence of "technical apparatuses" and bureaucratic forms of organization.

In 1932, the main work of existential philosophy PHILOSOPHIE was published with the three volumes PHILOSOPHISCHE WELTORIENTIERUNG, (PHILOSOPHICAL WORLDORIENTATION), EXISTENZERHELLUNG (EXISTENTIAL ELUCIDATION) and METAPHYSIK (METAPHYSICS). With this work, Jaspers established his reputation as one of the two most important German existential philosophers alongside Heidegger.

In 1935 and 1938 he published two more collections of lectures, VERNUNFT UND EXISTENZ (REASON AND EXISTENCE) and EXISTENZPHILOSOPHIE (PHILOSOPHY OF EXISTENCE), before he was banned from publishing by the National Socialists. In the first of these publications, he expanded his existential philosophy by placing ever greater emphasis on the concept of reason.

1.5   The Shock of the Nazi Dictatorship

IN 1930, when Jaspers wrote DIE GEISTIGE SITUATION DER ZEIT, in which he criticized tendencies toward the leveling and massification of individuals, he still knew "very little about National Socialism" and considered its "madness in Germany to be impossible".(Aut 72) All the greater then was his shock and dismay at the experiences he had to make during the Nazi dictatorship.

> What is possible to men in monstrosity, what is possible to the mentally gifted in delusion, what is possible to apparently good citizens in disloyalty, what is possible to the apparently proper man in wickedness, what is possible to the multitude in thoughtlessness, selfish, short-sighted passivity, became real to such an extent that the knowledge of man had to become different. (Aut 72)

After the onset of National Socialist rule, Jaspers was initially expelled from the university administration in 1933. In 1937 he was forced into retirement, and from 1938 onwards he was unofficially banned from publishing his writings by being deprived of the paper allocation for printing them, and from 1943 onwards he was officially banned from publishing them. Jaspers reports on the oppressive psychological climate and the life-threatening mode of existence under the Nazi regime in a biography that he had to write for the French military government after the end of this regime before resuming his teaching activities:

> A complete concealment of one's actual opinion, openness only among one's closest friends, a defensive way of speaking in generalities, a contradiction against accusations, in the decisive moment before the Gestapo the confession of one's own loyalty, the oath to Hitler in the summer of 1934 – which the entire academic corporation, including the Jews still in office at the time, took in an unceremonious mass action – the silence in the face of growing indignation and the foreboding of coming disaster, – all this brought about a state of mind that one felt to be deeply unworthy and yet could not change. Every attempt at resistance led only to self-destruction, according to Goebbels: "We let the mice out of their holes, watch them for a while, and then beat them to death". We had only one hope: liberation from the outside.[13]

The fact that his wife was of Jewish origin meant a heavy psychological burden for both of them. They had to expect daily that Mrs. Jaspers would be picked up by the Gestapo (Secret State Police) and deported to a concentration camp. Jaspers bravely withstood massive pressure from Nazi institutions to dissolve the frowned-upon "racially mixed marriage" and to separate from his wife. He carried a cyanide capsule with him at all times so that they could commit suicide together if she were deported to a concentration camp. A diary entry from 16.11.1939 reads:

> Gertrud keeps coming up with the thought: she alone wants to die, she does not want to destroy me at the same time – my death torments her, not hers. She wants permission from me to leave the world alone. But I cannot suffer her to die without me. Powers that force her to die kill me too. This solidarity is absolute. (SchW 158)

Offers to emigrate, which Jaspers received from Paris at the instigation first of *Lucien Lévy-Bruhl* and then of *Jean Wahl* (professor at the Sorbonne since 1927)[14] before France was occupied by the German "Wehrmacht", could not be accepted because of his unstable state of health. He and his wife agreed that he would not survive the stress and strain of the move under the conditions. Regarding the physical and emotional strain on the couple in Heidelberg during the Nazi dictatorship, a confidante of the couple reports that Mrs. Jaspers often had to hide overnight with friends in Heidelberg. This was the case when the danger of being picked up and taken away by the Gestapo during one of the many night and fog operations was very great. Jaspers and his wife were unable to visit his elderly parents in Oldenburg because it was no longer possible for them to spend the night in a Frankfurt hotel as a stopover. Hotel-stays had been generally forbidden for Jewish people since 1938. As the war continued, living conditions became more and more burdensome. A former student of Jaspers reports:

> Particularly difficult for Mrs. Professor was the procurement of milk. Because of his bronchitis, Jaspers was supposed to drink one and a half liters of milk a day. But no one was

---

[13] Karl Jaspers, Karl Heinrich Bauer, *Briefwechsel 1945–1968*, Heidelberg 1983, 5–6.
[14] Cf. Jean-Claude Gens, Zur Jaspers-Rezeption in der französischen Philosophie und Psychiatrie. In: *Jb. der Österreichischen Karl-Jaspers-Gesellschaft*, 26 (2013), 72.

allowed more than half a litre on prescription, and Jaspers did not get any more … Clothes, shoes, stockings and other articles of daily use had long since ceased to exist. All factories had been converted to war production. Coal was also scarce. Jaspers sat at his desk, his feet in a large fur sack, the elbows in his jacket mended, never saying a word about his limited circumstances. With the inadequate heating, it was no wonder that the Herr Professor caught pneumonia in the winter of 1941/1942.[15]

Towards the end of the war, the Jaspers' lived in constant danger. As Jaspers later learned, the deportation of all remaining Jewish people in Heidelberg to a concentration camp was scheduled for 14th April 1945.[16] Fortunately, the Americans occupied Heidelberg on 1st April 1945. After the collapse of the Nazi regime, Jaspers participated in the organizational reconstruction of Heidelberg University, where he chose as the topic of his first lecture the question of guilt and responsibility of the German people for the Nazi regime.

At the reopening of Heidelberg University on 15 August 1946, he gave a speech with the following thoughtful and perhaps self-critical passage:

> We survivors did not seek death. We did not go out into the streets when our Jewish friends were taken away, we did not scream until they destroyed us too. We preferred to stay alive with the weak, though correct, reason that our deaths could not have helped anything. That we live is our fault. We know before God what humbles us deeply. (RAu 130)

The experience of the Nazi dictatorship made Jaspers a political man, who from then on also took a public stand on day-to-day political issues.

Many colleagues and numerous readers of his works in Germany were disappointed when he accepted a professorship at the University of Basel in February 1948 at the age of 64. In the difficult phase of the reconstruction of a liberal-democratic German state, they felt abandoned by the very thinker who, only a short time before, in his book DIE SCHULDFRAGE (THE QUESTION OF GUILT), had evoked the intellectual and moral forces of a better, non-nationalistic Germanness.

The motivation for accepting the appointment to Basel is reported by *Edgar Salin, a* friend from early Heidelberg days. He was later a social scientist in Basel, who had a great influence on the appointment to Basel and also helped Jaspers to move there:

> But he was deeply shocked, not only by everything that had happened during the Nazi period, but also, and perhaps even more so, by the fact that the survivors had no sense of guilt and that he failed to awaken it in a large number of Germans, least of all colleagues. He, who so readily saw only the good of the people around him, fell into sad rage when he spoke of the lack of character of the most distinguished scholars in 1933, and of the even

---

[15] Wilhelmine Drescher, *Erinnerungen an Karl Jaspers in Heidelberg,* Meisenheim am Glan 1975, 39–40.

[16] Cf. Hans Saner, Überleben mit einer Jüdin in Deutschland. Karl und Gertrud Jaspers in der Zeit des Nationalsozialismus. In: ders, *Erinnern und Vergessen. Essays zur Geschichte des Denkens,* Basel 2004, 127.

more embarrassing way in which the same "March Fallen" were now struggling to obtain "Persil notes."[17]

Jaspers himself commented shortly before his death on the reasons for his departure from Heidelberg at that time:

> What drove us away was clear: the absence of the consequences of the mass murder of Jews – the radical distance from the total criminal state – my isolation in university endeavors – the hostility of the government – an overexposure to futile efforts – a diminution of the strength of my philosophical work. (SchW 180)

This echoes the disappointment that the construction of the Federal Republic and the re-establishment of the German universities did not bring about the radical "intellectual and moral conversion" or the radical "change in the way of thinking" that he had hoped for after the catastrophe of National Socialism. Another reason for the move to Basel, as *Hans Saner* has told me, was that Mrs. Jaspers was plagued by nightmares even after the end of the war. She dreamt that in the night there was a knock on the door of her Heidelberg house and that she and her husband would be picked up by the Gestapo and deported to a concentration camp.

There are several answers to the question of why Jaspers was able to survive the Nazi regime at all with his Jewish wife. *Saner* said:

> The fact that he was a prominent man who was also respected in Italy and Japan will also have protected him from the Nazis' quick grab. To a good extent, however, it was the merit of his shrewdness. Knowing his vital conditions, he gained clarity about the principles of perseverance that were valid for him. Since active resistance could be out of the question at all, it was pointless from the outset to use life wantonly, unless he had intended for himself the role of martyr and for his wife that of victim. He did not do so, but chose life for himself and his wife, on condition, however, that it was a common and not an undignified life. By this choice it was valid for him not to fall prey to the terror apparatus out of negligence, but to withdraw from it as far as possible. This withdrawal was easy for him inwardly, and by caution and silence also outwardly. There is no false public word from Jaspers from the years of the Nazi era, and he never gave in to the pressure to announce his agreement with National Socialism through a public act.[18]

1.6   From Existential Philosophy to the Philosophy of Reason and Politics

From 1950 onwards, when he published VERNUNFT UND WIDERVERNUNFT IN UNSERER ZEIT (REASON AND ANTI-REASON IN OUR TIME), Jaspers no longer wanted his philosophy to be understood as existential philosophy, but as philosophy of reason (cf. VWZ 40). After the book DIE SCHULDFRAGE, he published the extensive

---

[17] Edgar Salin, Freundschaftliche Erinnerungen an Karl Jaspers. In: Klaus Piper, Hans Saner (eds.), *Erinnerungen an Karl Jaspers,* 17.

[18] Hans Saner, Überleben mit einer Jüdin in Deutschland. Karl und Gertrud Jaspers in der Zeit des Nationalsozialismus. In: ders.:ebd., 127–129.

work Von der Wahrheit (Of Truth) in 1947, which was meant as the first volume of a new philosophical logic. The other three volumes (Kategorienlehre, Methodenlehre and Wissenschaftslehre) never appeared. With Von der Wahrheit, Jaspers aimed at "practicing reason as a basic philosophical attitude" (W 11) and making people aware of "ways of being". These, in a doctrine of "encompassing being" ("Periechontology") [Greek: periéchon: the encompassing], form the main theme of the book. The next book, Vom Ursprung und Ziel der Geschichte (the Origin and Goal of History), appeared in 1949, shortly after his move to Basel. It deals with the question of whether there is a structure in world history. The examination of religious faith viewpoints found expression in the books Der philosophische Glaube (1948) (PHILOSOPHICAL FAITH) and Der philosophische Glaube angesichts der Offenbarung (1962) (PHILOSOPHICAL FAITH AND REVELATION). Here Jaspers developed the concept of a *philosophical faith* as an alternative to confessional, religious faiths in revelation.

As far as Jaspers' publications on politics are concerned, the book Die Atombombe und die Zukunft des Menschen (1958) (THE ATOMBOMB AND THE FUTURE OF MAN) is the main work. Public statements on current political events in the Federal Republic of Germany appeared in the books Freiheit und Wiedervereinigung. Über Aufgaben deutscher Politik (1960), FREEDOM AND REUNIFICATION. ON THE TASKS OF GERMAN POLITICS), Hoffnung und Sorge. Schriften zur deutschen Politik 1945–1965 (1965) (HOPE AND CONCERN. WRITINGS ABOUT GERMAN POLICY 1945–1965) and Wohin treibt die Bundesrepublik? Tatsachen – Gefahren – Chancen (1966). (WHERE IS THE FEDERAL REPUBLIC DRIFTING? FACTS – DANGERS – CHANCES). These works are discussed in detail here in Chap. 9.

In tireless work during his academic career, Jaspers also wrote books on the classics of the history of philosophy: thus a Nietzsche and a Descartes- book (1936 and 1937), as well as books on Schelling (1955) and Nicolaus Cusanus (1964). Already in a retrospective and outlook on his life's work, he mentions the project of a "universal history of philosophy" as his "concluding life's project". Of this project, however, only the volume Die grossen Philosophen (1957) (THE GREAT PHILOSOPHERS) appeared. Important parts of this gigantic project were found in Jaspers' estate after his death and edited by *Saner* in a double volume Die grossen Philosophen, Nachlass 1 und 2 (1981).

1.7 Appealing Teaching as a Lifelong Challenge

Accounts of Jaspers' teaching activities show that he always held his lectures in front of full lecture halls and often in the auditorium maximum of Heidelberg University. As a teacher, he must have made a fascinating impression on students. Already his physiognomy – a slender tall figure and body height of over 1.90 m – attracted attention. A student sensitive to physiognomic impressions describes the impression he made on his first visit to a lecture:

A tall, slender figure, with a strikingly noble head and clear, deeply gazing eyes, with a quite calm but nevertheless deeply exciting voice, appeared on the lectern ... and from the first moment I was captivated, excited, "addressed" – although I thought I understood almost nothing at first ... . This *man* Karl Jaspers attracted me by a tremendous seriousness of his being and the content of "his" philosophy, and although at first I stood stunned before a completely new spiritual world, I was affected to the innermost: ... This man convinced me that he *lived* what he presented.[19]

The impression that Jaspers lived what he presented points to the understanding of philosophy that decisively shaped his existential philosophy. Philosophy should not merely be the design of rational systems, as he exemplarily saw in his colleague in Heidelberg, the Neukantian *Heinrich Rickert* and his efforts to create a system of values. For Jaspers, philosophizing should be a personally engaged thought and appealing action that must find its expression in one's personal attitude and conduct of life. The appeal to students to philosophize should at the same time be an appeal to set in motion the process of self-reflection, which points to the possibility of one's own selfhood (one's own realization of existence).

Among Jaspers' female students, the philosopher *Jeanne Hersch, in* addition to *Hannah Arendt,* has achieved international renown. She contributed a great deal to making Jaspers known in the French-speaking world. She describes her first impression on attending a Jaspers lecture as follows:

It was in the auditorium of the old university (Heidelberg, K.S.). I was sitting in a window niche on the side. When Jaspers began to speak, he raised his hand. Never will I forget that moment, that voice, that hand ... I understood nothing. I had stumbled into the middle of a lecture, understood the language poorly, and had almost no previous knowledge of philosophy. Nevertheless, my innermost being was full of joy, because that much I understood, that there was something to understand here....[20]

Jaspers' teaching method is described by *Hersch* thus:

The teaching activity of Jaspers ... never granted satisfaction. No sooner did one find joy in a new intellectual achievement than it was snatched away from one with severity ... One was thrown from one thought to another, from enthusiasm to restriction, from impossibility to demand, and the philosophical call resounded through all thoughts ... In all this there was something firm, unshakable: one saw a man who based himself on truth – and on it alone.[21]

Michael Landmann, who was an assistant to Jaspers in Basel from 1947 to 1951 before being appointed to the FU Berlin (Free University Berlin), gives the following description of his impression of Jaspers' lectures:

A beguiling melody ran through his lectures. As rational as every word he spoke was, his voice betrayed that he had not only gained it rationally. This voice still came from a deeper

---

[19] Heinrich Liepmann, Erinnerungen an Karl Jaspers aus den Jahren 1925–1936. In: Klaus Piper, Hans Saner (eds.), *Erinnerungen an Karl Jaspers,* 48.

[20] Jeanne Hersch, Karl Jaspers as Teacher. In: *Offener Horizont. Festschrift für Karl Jaspers,* ed. by Klaus Piper, München 1953, 440.

[21] Jeanne Hersch, ibid., 442.

layer, and therefore awakened in the listener more than mere intellectual comprehension. Here stood not only one who can think, but a man who is philosophically excited as a whole, for whom thought forms only the brightest tip of an elementary philosophical nature.[22]

As peculiarities of Jaspers' teaching activity can be gathered from the recollections of former students: a strict insistence on punctuality. Jaspers was enraged if someone did not appear punctually for the lectures and at the specified time in his office hours. If someone was late for a lecture, he would interrupt in mid-sentence until there was complete silence in the lecture hall again. Jaspers was also used to keeping strict time limits in his own life (e.g. three quarters of an hour to work, a quarter of an hour to rest, strictly regulated times for meals and for coughing up lung secretions).

When it came to working out the thoughts of the classics of philosophy in the seminar, Jaspers was an opponent of reading secondary literature. He is said to have said: *"One book by Kant* is much better than a hundred books *about Kant."* One can only get to know the great philosophers at their source, i.e. from the original texts.[23]

Having come to philosophy himself by way of medicine and psychology, and having had no school-based philosophical training, he wanted neither to found a philosophical school nor to have students who wanted to become his pupils. *Gerhard Knauss* problematizes this attitude by asking: did the idea of a school really contradict his idea of philosophy? Or was he perhaps too shy to attract people to himself? Did he not regret in his old age that he had no students who would try to systematically develop his philosophy in his name? *Knauss,* who wrote his doctoral thesis under Jaspers, writes about his personal impressions, among other things:

> He was implacably strict with us students. He did not forgive tardiness … A lecture had the severity of a mess, the seminar outwardly resembled an exam. The discipline he practiced himself and demanded of others bordered on pedantry. But in the matter he was singularly tolerant. The thing, that is, philosophical thought. I know of no instance where he rejected a paper or dissertation because he disagreed with its content. His tolerance was not indiscriminate acceptance, but a sense of what was important, even if it forced him to self-correct.[24]

Knauss describes personal conversations with Jaspers alone or in a small circle at Jaspers' home as follows:

> What one said was weighed. One was not allowed to speak into the unclean, not even to joke and let oneself be carried away by moods. Alcohol and tobacco were proscribed in his environment anyway. I wonder if he had a sense of humor. I never noticed it. He could tell

---

[22] Michael Landmann, Erinnerungen an Karl Jaspers. In: Klaus Piper, Hans Saner (eds.), *Erinnerungen an Karl Jaspers,* 196.

[23] Cf. Liepmann, ibid., 50.

[24] Gerhard Knauss, Erinnerungen an Karl Jaspers. In: Klaus Piper, Hans Saner (eds.), *Erinnerungen an Karl Jaspers,* 168.

jokes, even in lecture, good jokes that I still remember. But they were never told for the sake of laughing; they always served to demonstrate a philosophical thought. Even when he laughed, he moralized with it. I never saw a man so in control of himself. Whether he intended to criticize or to praise one, he always received one with the same cool friendliness. He tried to go easy on us young people. He often postponed harsh criticism from the seminar to office hours in order to spare the person concerned public embarrassment.[25]

A similar characterization of Jaspers' personality can be found in *Golo Mann*'s memoirs of his youth, when he asks himself whether Jaspers was a happy person and comes to the conclusion:

Satisfied with himself, he was fair to others, with himself also. He rejoiced in the successes of his books, the moral, the commercial. He loved his wife, … he loved Hannah Arendt. But much joy in life had not been given him, for which his illness alone was not to blame. He had devoted his life exclusively to his work, disciplined it for her … I cannot imagine him laughing heartily, not at "small talk", not at harmless card games or telling jokes.[26]

In the recollections of students, the visit to Jaspers' home is described very positively. Jaspers often invited students to visit him. They usually followed the following ritual: after ringing the house bell, Mrs. Jaspers opened the front door, greeted the guest with selected friendliness, and engaged the student in a short conversation before escorting him or her into the study of "Herr Professor". There one could take a seat in a comfortable leather chair and present one's concerns and philosophical questions to Jaspers.

For Jaspers, personal dialogue with students had a special significance; he avoided group discussions whenever possible. He was a patient and attentive listener when presenting the results of his thinking in a dialogue, before he calmly and non-authoritatively brought his own interpretative hypotheses to the students' attention. Only in late life did he become, as *Knauss* notes with regard to teaching in Basel, more intolerant and opinionated. A former doctoral student reports on his conversation experience from the earlier Heidelberg period:

Already after the first sentences I felt that I was not sitting opposite a teacher who lectures in an authoritarian manner, but a teacher who challenges the student to think for himself in communication.[27]

That the impressions of former students reproduced here are to be seen in the context of a certain philosophy of education, which Jaspers advocated in his writing DIE IDEE DER UNIVERSITÄT (THE IDEA OF THE UNIVERSITY), but also scattered in other works, will become clear here in Chap. 4.

---

[25] Ibid., 166.

[26] Cf. Golo Mann, *Erinnerungen und Gedanken. Eine Jugend in Deutschland,* Frankfurt a. M. 1986, 331–332.

[27] Julius Löwenstein: Erinnerungen an Jaspers. In: Klaus Piper, Hans Saner (eds.), *Erinnerungen an Karl Jaspers,* 44.

How strongly Jaspers was influenced by an Enlightenment ethos throughout his life is demonstrated by the following passage in his AUTOBIOGRAPHIE:

> In my writings, which are written throughout in calm objectivity, lives a will to have an effect: to do what is possible to promote reason in the world to a tiny degree, but to do so in such a way as to cause the reader anxiety by arousing his possible existence, to encourage him in becoming himself, to conjure up for him the possible meaning in being, and to leave him thinking stranded in the incomprehensible. It is a tendency ... in which I stand, for which and with which I think, to which I would like to encourage others. (Aut 134–135)

The extent to which Jaspers was keen to convey his philosophical messages and moral appeals to as many people as possible is demonstrated by his receptiveness to new media at the time. His publisher *Klaus Piper* noted:

> Jaspers wanted to be read, he wanted to have an effect. He affirmed all technical possibilities to make his books – his thinking and the substance of the personal life experience from which it stems – accessible to the readers of "mass society". Without suspicion, without hesitation, he made use of the modern media of radio and television.[28]

The writer and dramatist *Rolf Hochhuth,* a personal friend of Jaspers in Basel, also praised this openness to the media:

> Jaspers was the first to philosophize on television for thirteen half hours with everyone – and when he emphasized: whoever thinks must "go out into the street" ...for the present, or for myself, it seemed self-evident to me that philosophy ultimately proves itself by generating impulses that can spread among the population.[29]

Jaspers' media friendliness was evident in numerous interviews with radio and television journalists. *Saner* later published these conversations as an anthology under the title PROVOKATIONEN. GESPRÄCHE UND INTERVIEWS (1969) (PROVOCATIONS. TALKS AND INTERVIEWS). The interviews were broadcast by Bayrischer Rundfunk, Norddeutscher Rundfunk, Studio Basel, or Swiss television, and by the television of North and West Germany. Among the most prominent journalists of his time who had public conversations with Jaspers on philosophical and political topics were *Willy Hochkeppel, Francois Bondy, Heinz Zahrnt, Peter Wyss, Thilo Koch.* A much-noticed interview for an article in "Der Spiegel" was conducted by *Rudolf Augstein.*

Jaspers worked on the planned world history of philosophy until the end of his life. It was to be the preliminary stage of a "world philosophy". He was unable to elaborate on this vision because his health deteriorated increasingly from 1965

---

[28] Klaus Piper, Karl Jaspers, Erinnerungen aus verlegerischer Zusammenarbeit. In: Klaus Piper, Hans Saner (eds.), *Erinnerungen an Karl Jaspers,* 191; cf. also: Dirk Fonfara, Einleitung. In: ders. (ed.), *Ausgewählte Verlags- und Übersetzerkorrespondenzen. In: Karl Jaspers Gesamtausgabe,* vol. III/8,1, Basel 2018, XXXV–XV.

[29] Rolf Hochhuth, Lebensfreundlichkeit. In: Klaus Piper, Hans Saner (eds.), *Erinnerungen an Karl Jaspers,* 297.

onwards. As *Saner* reports in his Jaspers monograph, Jaspers suffered from intestinal bleeding, arthritis, atrophy of the upper and lower leg muscles, and attacks of rheumatism. In 1968 he suffered a mild stroke. On his 86th birthday, 23 February 1969, "he received for the last time some friends, to whom he signified, physically labored but without emotion, that he would not live much longer."[30]

He died in Basel on 26th February 1969 at the age of 86. This day was his wife's 90th birthday. His urn was buried there at the Hörnli cemetery. Two years before his death, Jaspers had taken Swiss citizenship.

---

[30] Hans Saner, *Karl Jaspers,* Reinbek 12th. ed. 2005, 67.

Encounter with Two Controversial Thinkers: Max Weber and Martin Heidegger

2

2.1 The Formative Encounter with Max Weber

In a personal review of his relationship with *Weber*, Jaspers writes of his deep admiration for the latter:

> On the winding paths that life forces us to take, Max Weber became for my wife and me again and again the exit of an irreplaceable reassurance. To think of him was like a guarantee even in dark hours. From him we could know what a human being is capable of, what reliability and depth of spirit is, what it is to be German. The question, what would Max Weber say, became a claim. The content of his being, once absorbed in youth, became an origin from which new things are always able to grow in a lifelong manner. (Ant 840)

Jaspers had known *Weber* since 1909, and for the longest time he was his great role model both as a personality and as a scholar and researcher. Weber's methodological insights, which decisively influenced Jaspers' scientific work, include the concepts of an understanding sociology, of ideal types in social science research, and of the value freedom principle in the empirical sciences.

This influence left clear traces in the first two books Jaspers published, the methodological book ALLGEMEINE PSYCHOPATHOLOGIE and the PSYCHOLOGIE DER WELTANSCHAUUNGEN. It can also be seen in a lecture Jaspers gave on "Contemporary Philosophy" in the winter semester of 1960/1961. There he presented *Weber* together with *Einstein* as the most important philosophers of the present.

> Max Weber has appeared to me as the real philosopher of the time, the philosopher who did not speak his philosophy directly, but lived and thought from it [...] For me, I can only point to the continuity of this view in me for 50 years – to the fact that my philosophizing has not happened all these years without thinking of Max Weber, – in the question: what would he say? – in the attribution of his basic position – not in the way of continuing his sociology and sociological research, but in the way of making this philosophizing conscious. Since 1909 I have been under his influence. (GP, N 1641–642)

Jaspers' esteem for *Weber* sometimes went so far as to call him the "intellectually greatest man" of the age and the "Galileo of the humanities" (cf. SchW 33). From

© Springer-Verlag GmbH Germany, part of Springer Nature 2022
K. Salamun, *Karl Jaspers*, https://doi.org/10.1007/978-3-476-05896-6_2

an ideological-philosophical point of view, Jaspers counted *Weber* among the "spirits of the first rank" who were always concerned about the freedom of the individual. The influence of *Weber* on Jaspers has been addressed by *Raymond Aron, Renato de Rosa* and *Dieter Henrich*, among others.[1]

Weber also played a significant role in Jaspers' academic career. With an expert opinion, he contributed to Jaspers being able to habilitate in psychology at the Faculty of Philosophy at the University of Heidelberg with the book ALLGEMEINE PSYCHOPATHOLOGIE. During occasional visits to the so-called "Weber Circle" in Heidelberg Jaspers met prominent scholars of his time such as *Georg Simmel, Emil Lask, Gustav Radbruch, Ernst Troeltsch* and others. When *Weber* died in 1920, Jaspers gave a memorial speech to the Heidelberg student body in which he praised *Weber* not merely as a sociologist, but as an "existential philosopher" who had exemplified "greatness", "truthfulness", "deep seriousness", "love of human beings", "self-sufficiency", "solitary steadfastness" and "unconditionality in action" with his life, political commitment and fragmentary work (cf. MW 9, 18, 22).

In 1932, Jaspers published a book entitled MAX WEBER. DEUTSCHES WESEN IM POLITISCHEN DENKEN, IM FORSCHEN UND PHILOSOPHIEREN (GERMAN ESSENCE IN POLITICAL THINKING, RESEARCH AND PHILOSOPHY), a book in which he pays tribute to *Weber* in three respects: as a politician, as a researcher and as a philosopher. After the Second World War, this book appeared in another edition under the amended title: MAX WEBER. POLITIKER, FORSCHER, PHILOSOPH. In the preface to this edition, Jaspers explains the use of the word "German essence" in the first edition as an attitude of opposition to the mystification of the "German essence" by National Socialism at that time (cf. also Jaspers 1988).

The fact that remarks about *Weber's* mental illness can be found in Jaspers' legacy can also be seen as evidence of how great Jaspers' interest in *Weber's* overall personality was, not least as a psychiatrist. He diagnosed the latter's mental problems not as an organic mental illness, but as a neurologically caused, "curable functional mental disorder, running unpredictably, in fluctuations." (GP, N 1, 649).

The unrestricted appreciation of *Weber's* personality was impaired when, in 1967, Jaspers came to read through *Eduard Baumgarten*, a relative of Weber, love letters to *Else Jaffé*, which *Weber* had written. The concealment of the love affair with *Else Jaffé* from Weber's wife *Marianne*, shook Jaspers' faith in the "boundless honesty" of his previous great role model to a considerable degree.[2]

---

[1] Cf. Raymond Aron, Karl Jaspers und die Politik. In: Jeanne Hersch et al. (eds.), *Karl Jaspers. Philosoph – Arzt – politischer Denker*, München 1996, 59–76; Renato de Rosa, Politische Akzente im Leben eines Philosophen. Karl Jaspers in Heidelberg 1901–1946. in: Nachwort zu ders. (ed.), *Karl Jaspers, Erneuerung der Universität. Reden und Schriften 1945/1946*, Heidelberg 1986, 314; Dieter Henrich, Denken im Hinblick auf Max Weber. In: ders. (Ed.), *Karl Jaspers: Max Weber. Gesammelte Schriften*, München, Zürich 1988, 7–31.

[2] Cf. Eduard Baumgarten, Zur Erinnerung an die Jaspers'sche Form Streitgespräche – feindlich und freundlich – fort und fort in Gang zu halten. In: Klaus Piper, Hans Saner (eds.), *Erinnerungen an Karl Jaspers*, 125; Renato De Rosa, op. cit., 328; Dieter Henrich, op. cit., 24–27.

2.2   The Ambivalent Relationship to Martin Heidegger

For Jaspers, *Heidegger* was initially a valued discussion partner. After *Heidegger's* commitment to National Socialism in 1933, he became an ambivalent personality for Jaspers and the antithesis to his own philosophical thinking. Jaspers met *Heidegger* in the spring of 1920 during a visit to *Heidegger's* teacher *Edmund Husserl* in Freiburg. Jaspers appreciated in *Heidegger*, who was seven years younger and at the beginning of his academic career, the ability to conduct intensive and profound philosophical conversations. Both were united in their rejection of established university philosophy, which at the time was represented by Neo-Kantianism. They saw each other as united in a "rare and distinct community of struggle" against university philosophy, as *Heidegger* put it in a letter to Jaspers.

When *Heidegger* traveled from Freiburg to other German university towns, especially Marburg, where he held a professorship between 1923 and 1927, he often stopped off in Heidelberg at the home of the Jaspers couple. Sometimes he stayed overnight there and "philosophized" for hours with the older professional colleague. Jaspers reports about these meetings:

> If Heidegger was visiting us, we both used to work. In the course of the day we met several times for conversations. Even the first conversations between us inspired me. One can hardly imagine the satisfaction I felt at being able to talk seriously at all with at least one person in the philosophers' guild … The common opposition to traditional professorial philosophy was clear. Unclear, but deeply moving, was the vague certainty that within the framework of professorial philosophy … something like a reversal was necessary. A renewal not of philosophy, but of the form of philosophy found at the universities at that time was what we both felt to be the task. Both of us were moved by Kierkegaard. (Aut 94)

Jaspers also acknowledged the fact that he owed *Heidegger* many insights into "the Christian, especially Catholic, tradition of thought" (such as that of Augustine and Thomas Aquinas) during the phase of his familiarization with the field of philosophy.

However, Jaspers later put the originally positive descriptions of his relationship with *Heidegger* into another perspective.

> From the beginning, our relationship had no streak of enthusiasm. It was not a friendship based on the depth of our being. Through external circumstances as well as through behavior and words, something distant was mixed in. Thus the mood between us was not clear, only in beautiful moments of conversation did it become pure and unreserved for hours. (Aut 96–97)

One is not wrong in assuming that the main reason for Jaspers' distancing was *Heidegger's* political commitment to National Socialism.[3]

During *Heidegger's* last visit in May 1933, *Heidegger's* National Socialist sentiments were revealed both in private conversation and in a public lecture at the

---

[3] Cf. the books: Karl Löwith, *Mein Leben in Deutschland vor und nach 1933. Ein Bericht*, Stuttgart 1986; Hugo Ott, *Martin Heidegger: unterwegs zu seiner Biographie*, New York 1988; Victor Farias, *Heidegger und der Nationalsozialismus*, Frankfurt 1989; Alexander Schwan, *Politische Philosophie im Denken Heideggers*, Opladen 2.ed. 1989.

university attended by Jaspers. The lecture was entitled "Die Universität im neuen Reich" (cf. Saner 1991, 172). Since this visit, Jaspers and *Heidegger* never met again.

Hannah Arendt, who was a student of *Heidegger*, tried to mediate between the two; she even had a love affair with him as a young student while he was teaching at the University of Marburg. But she was also a dissertation student of Jaspers, with whom she submitted her doctoral thesis on the *"Liebesbegriff bei Augustinus" (The Concept of Love in Augustine)* at Heidelberg in 1927. She tried to bring the two back into contact several times after the war, but in vain. In a letter to her husband *Heinrich Blücher, Arendt* refers to a misunderstanding on both sides: Jaspers assumed that *Heidegger* no longer wanted to visit him because of his Jewish wife; *Heidegger* was ashamed of his original enthusiasm for National Socialism and therefore shied away from a personal encounter.[4]

The ambivalent relationship between Jaspers and *Heidegger* is also characterized by the following facts: After the end of the Nazi regime, Jaspers was asked for an expert opinion on *Heidegger* in December 1945 by the so-called Purification Commission of the University of Freiburg. This Commision had to obtain expert opinions for the French military government of Baden on the dismissal or reinstatement of professors to the teaching staff. Jaspers wrote this report very soon, and in it he proposed that *Heidegger* be granted a personal pension so that he could continue his philosophical work and publish his writings, but that he should be excluded from the teaching staff of the university. Significant passages from this report are:

Heidegger is a significant potency, not by the content of a philosophical worldview, but in the handling of speculative tools. He has a philosophical organ whose perceptions are interesting, although in my opinion he is unusually uncritical and far removed from actual science. In the current of his linguistics he is occasionally able to strike the nerve of philosophizing in a hidden and magnificent way. Here, as far as I can see, he is perhaps the only one among contemporary philosophers in Germany. ...Thus it is inevitable that those who helped to lift National Socialism into the saddle should be called to account. Heidegger is one of the few professors who did that.

...What, if Heidegger remains unrestricted, are those colleagues to say who have to leave, who are in need, and who have never committed National Socialist acts! The unusual intellectual achievement can be a justifiable reason for continuing this work, but not for continuing office and teaching. ...Heidegger's way of thinking, which seems to me to be by its very nature unfree, dictatorial, lacking in communication, would be disastrous in its teaching effect today ... As long as a genuine rebirth does not take place in him, which is visibly at work, I do not think that such a teacher can be placed before the youth, who today are inwardly almost unresisting. First the youth must come to independent thinking.[5]

However, four years later Jaspers wrote to the then Rector of the University of Freiburg:·

---

[4] Cf. Hannah Arendt, Heinrich Blücher, *Briefe 1936–1968*, München 1996, 225.

[5] Martin Heidegger, Karl Jaspers, *Briefwechsel 1920–1963*, Frankfurt, München, Zürich 1990, 271–272.

The time seems ripe to me now. In my opinion, the German university can no longer leave
Heidegger on the sidelines. I therefore warmly support the motion to invest Heidegger with
the rights of an emeritus professor.[6]

Heidegger was officially allowed to resume teaching in the winter semester of
1950/1951.

If we look at the correspondence between the two, which continued after 1945
with longer interruptions, it is noticeable, in addition to the always friendly tone of
conversation, that neither of the two commented on the books and writings written
by the other. The main themes of the letters are, before 1933, the raising of the standard of dissertations, the fundamental reform of universities, and the renewal of
philosophy in the sense of a specialized discipline that transcends the narrower,
scientific way of thinking. Almost throughout, there are evaluations of professional
colleagues and opinions on which professorship at which university one or the other
was better suited for.

Despite a break in personal contact, it can be said that Jaspers was intellectually
engaged with *Heidegger's* personality and philosophical style of thought for a large
part of his life. The extensive NACHLASS contained numerous notes that he had put
down on paper about *Heidegger* between the years 1928 and 1964 and stacked on
his desk. These notes were first published in book form by Jaspers' executor *Saner*
in 1978 under the title: NOTIZEN ZU MARTIN HEIDEGGER (NOTICES ABOUT
HEIDEGGER). The latter writes about them:

These notes, some 300 sheets dating from 1928–1964, were on Jaspers' desk at the time of
his death. Although he had not worked on them for almost five years, they were ready to
hand, as if the 'conversation' could be resumed at any time.[7]

The notes often only fragment, but very clearly reflect the ambivalent impression
that *Heidegger* made on Jaspers, both as a person and with his philosophizing. The
notes are informative insofar as they reflect a deep mistrust: a mistrust that Jaspers,
from the background of his liberal-Enlightenment training in *Kant and Weber*, must
have had towards a philosophizing that, in the style of a prophecy of salvation and
suggestive word creations, conjures up a history of being that ultimately remains in
the numinous. It is clear from some of these notes that Jaspers, due to his liberal
mindset, must also have perceived *Heidegger's* thinking, which in his view was
dogmatic and associated with implicit claims to power, as politically dangerous.

As for the style of philosophizing, Jaspers accuses *Heidegger* of the following:
his methods of mixing poetry, philosophy, and science are "methods of justifying
confusion and fog, preparations of a generation of the kind of thinking that are ready
to fall into totalitarianism." (NH 80); principled questioning relativizes and negates
from a point of reference *Heidegger* calls "Being." This point of reference, however,

---

[6] Jaspers, ibid., 276.
[7] Hans Saner, Abwehr und Huldigung. Zu den Plänen einer wechselseitigen Kritik von Heidegger
und Jaspers. In: ders, *Einsamkeit und Kommunikation. Essays zur Geschichte des Denkens*, Basel
1994, 189.

remains "dark" and is "suitable for negation" but offers no reference to the "present-ness of my life,…no reference to ethos" (NH 64); *Heidegger's* philosophizing is "a foreboding speaking, announcing itself in hint and promise, – ambiguous, – obscur-ing" (NH 83); he engages in a "magization of language" (NH 142) and thus pro-duces "not self-thinking, not freedom, – but aesthetic bias." (NH 157); *Heidegger*, with the "total critique of being-historical, which goes into the fantastic of a mysti-fying whole, misses the real critique, which has factual-scientific and existential relevance." (NH 215); "As a philosopher, he actually wanted to educate the Führer." (NH 187); the "language of Heidegger's N.S. speeches," here obviously meaning speeches by *Heidegger* as National Socialist Rector of the University of Freiburg, is the same as in his philosophy. "It shows itself to be hollow, from afar reminiscent of Hitler, taking up turns of Hitler, in this line linguistically perpetuating in constant untruthfulness." (NH 240); the way of thinking of those "who seized National Socialism with enthusiasm" persisted only in other "clothes" unchanged in *Heidegger's* philosophy, "the dictatorial, the assertive, the thinking oneself superior, the one alone true, the inclination to the absurd, the primary aggressiveness, nega-tion, the will to power." (NH 267) Notes that Jaspers formulated in the form of questions are no less critical and polemical, here are several examples:

Is Heidegger a creator in the sense of the uncontrolled? – Did he put into the world entities and visions that are true? – Or is there too much mimicry in them?
   That is a question that cannot be answered objectively. To me it has worked in sparks that belong there, tiny, but then perverted by artificial fires, by straw fires without substance. (NH 236)

Is it a sophisticated way of saying you have nothing to say? (in a distant analogy to mystics).
   And is this precisely what some people want to hear, that there is nothing to say?
   Is this nothingness the void into which everything can enter: self-will, – justification of the arbitrary, – destruction, – Nazism, Bolshevism? – and also the old ecclesiasticism?
   Is this emptiness beneficial because it is non-committal, – and then because it is capable of provoking and justifying the totalitarian of every shape?
   Is the dictatorial tone audible from the outset in this speaking, which attracts as a tone precisely when it commands nothing in the constant commanding? (NH 160)

Always the question for us (since 'Being and Time') about: 'determination', but to what end? Emptiness finds fulfillment in National Socialism. 'Shepherd of being' and 'place-holder of nothing' – but what is being and nothing but the pointer into the mystery at all? Arbitrariness in the practice of human existence –, lack of leadership or dictatorship – absence of reason and existence – … The doctrine that teaches nothing except the way to say this nothing in a way that is magnificent in its way: the great art of saying that he has nothing to say. (NH 176)

Even from the point of view of *Saner*, who as Jaspers' personal assistant for many years knew his character structure well, these extremely negative characterizations of *Heidegger* appear to be incompatible with Jaspers' other "nobility" and "sovereignty".
   Jaspers also reflects briefly on his reaction to *Heidegger's* writings in these notes and in the chapter on *Heidegger* that he included only after the latter's death in the

expanded new edition (1977) of the AUTOBIOGRAPHIE, saying that he did not react
to them "inwardly." About *Heidegger's* standard work SEIN UND ZEIT (1928)
(BEING AND TIME), which made the latter world-famous, it says there:

> Now I saw a work that immediately made an impression through the intensity of its elabora-
> tion, the constructiveness of its terminology, and the accuracy of its often illuminating new
> use of words. Despite the brilliance of its powerful analysis, however, it seemed to me
> unproductive for what I desired philosophically. I rejoiced in the achievement of the man
> associated with me, but was reluctant to read it, soon getting stuck because style, content,
> and mode of thought did not appeal to me. (Aut 98–99)

In one of the unpublished notes, Jaspers writes about this book that he had read little
of it. It seemed to him to "not have much to do" with what he thought he had "in
common" with *Heidegger.* In *Heidegger's* writings he had admittedly "sensed
echoes" of his own philosophizing, because in them he could see similarities of
origin to *Kierkegaard, Nietzsche, Hegel, Meister Eckhardt and Plotinus.* In comparison to how he himself had appropriated the thinking of these philosophers, in
Heidegger's case there had been "as it were a distorting mirroring of that tradition"
(cf. NH 233).

One can ask several questions in light of these extremely negative remarks,
which Jaspers never published: From what motives did Jaspers' pejorative judgments result? Was it experiences of dishonesty that Jaspers experienced on the part
of *Heidegger*, when *Heidegger* denied negative judgments about Jaspers' philosophy in lectures during personal confrontations with Jaspers? In this context, two
passages from letters by *Hannah Arendt* to her husband *Heinrich Blücher* also seem
noteworthy:

> His letters to Jaspers, which he gave me to read, all as before: the same mixture of genuine-
> ness and mendacity, or rather cowardice, both being equally original.[8]

In a letter of 08.02.1950 she says in reference to *Heidegger*: "And he, who after all
notoriously lies always and everywhere, wherever he can …".[9]

Or was it *Heidegger's* confession of National Socialism that must have deeply
affected Jaspers because of his wife's Jewish origin? Or was it also the popularity
and worldwide reception of *Heidegger's* philosophy that far exceeded the international response to Jaspers' philosophy? Could Jaspers not bear the fact that, although
he was considered, along with *Heidegger*, to be the main exponent of German existential philosophy, he always remained "in Heidegger's shadow" in terms of public
resonance? Why did Jaspers want the Heidegger chapter in his AUTOBIOGRAPHIE
published until after the latter's death? Was he not courageous enough for a public
confrontation?

Perhaps it is interesting to consider the judgment of Jaspers' student *Jeanne
Hersch* on Jaspers' relationship to Heidegger:

---

[8] Letter from 03.01.1950.
[9] Hannah Arendt, Heinrich Blücher, *Briefe 1936–1968*, München 1996, 190, 208.

Jaspers never had unqualified trust in Heidegger – not the kind of trust he calls *communication* in his work ... For Jaspers, all genuine philosophical activity is anchored in an ethical, indeed almost meta-ethical attitude at the existential level, that is, in that on which ethics itself is founded ... Well, that was not the case with Heidegger ... Jaspers recognized in him the gift of metaphysical introspection, but which lacked existential commitment.[10]

Hersch's judgment about A ABOUT *Heidegger*, with whom she herself had attended lectures in Freiburg in 1933, is similar to that of Jaspers:

I think there are passages in Heidegger's philosophy that lend themselves to all kinds of compromises. It carries something pathetic, more or less magical, that leads to irresponsibility. Jaspers has always sensed this, even when the two were friends. The poetic-magical side of Heidegger's thinking was also felt in the way he taught. The thoughts he developed were not proposed to our judgment, as befits the liberal attitude of a philosopher. He thrust them upon us. His philosophy contains something like incantations that make the earth spirits rise up and require one to submit to them.[11]

---

[10] Gabriell Dufour, Alfred Dufour, *Schwierige Freiheit. Gespräche mit Jeanne Hersch*, München, Zürich 1990, 36–37.

[11] Ibid., 35.

What Is the Meaning of Being Human?

3

3.1 The Human Being and the Antinomian Basic Structure of Existence

For Jaspers, being human is a never-completed process of realizing the possibilities of individual selfhood. The effort for world orientation, self-elucidation and the consideration of a being that transcends all objective thinking can never be completed. The dynamic basic tendency of individual life completion belongs to the anthropological structure of human beings. Jaspers has expressed this in the form of metaphors by referring to being human as being permanently "on the way". A medieval verse that he quoted at the end of his farewell lecture in the summer semester of 1961 at the University of Basel reads:

> I come, I know not whence, I die, I know not when, I go, I know not whither, I wonder that I am merry. (Ch 112)

The basic dynamic tendency is also evident from the metaphor of the "housings" of worldviews (cf. PW 281–284, 304–327).[1] Jaspers sees life as determined by two constantly repeated activities: the construction of "rational housings" and the relativization of such housings. He assumes that deeply embedded in the psychophysical structure of human beings is a primary drive for unity, closure, calm, security, and safety (cf. PW 304). This drive necessarily leads to the formation of rational housings in the form of objective worldviews, schematized ways of life, generally binding rules, social and legal institutions, etc. Every human being needs a stable worldview that remains constant over time as an orientation aid. This is the prerequisite for arranging the diversity of experiences and for gaining a certain degree of behavioral security in the world through rational reduction of complexity. In addition to this positive function, however, Jaspers also sees the danger of dogmatization associated with rational worldviews. If worldviews are dogmatized into rational

---

[1] Cf: Harald Stelzer, Von Max Weber's Gehäuse-Metapher zum Gehäuse-Begriff bei Karl Jaspers. In: *Studia Philosophica*, 67 (2008), 301–322.

© Springer-Verlag GmbH Germany, part of Springer Nature 2022
K. Salamun, *Karl Jaspers*, https://doi.org/10.1007/978-3-476-05896-6_3

housings (cages) they restrict individual freedom and creative spontaneity. They reduce the possibilities in which man can realize his individual and unjustifiable self through personal self-determination. Therefore, there must always be a second, counteracting activity at work in the psycho-structure: the effort to re-relate or "break up" rational enclosures and systems of categorization. The point is,

> ... to question and not take for granted any enclosure in which we live, but conversely to presuppose that it will be only *one* possibility among others. (PW 142)

The dialectic between construction and destruction, construction and dismantling, fixation and relativization of rational worldviews, systems of rules, institutions, etc., which on the one hand offer security and support in the life process, but on the other hand kill off what is specifically human (free decision of will, personal responsibility, creative impulses), is necessarily part of the conditio humana. In this the "antinomian basic structure" of man and of being in general manifests itself. This basic structure conditions are the "inevitable opposites within us." (PW 238).

3.2   The Human Being as Empirical Ego or Objectifiable Existence

The antinomian structure of the human being is expressed in the fact that being human is realized in two different dimensions of being. These are the "empirical ego" and the "true selfhood" or "existence". Via the empirical ego, descriptions and explanations can be given, as well as generally valid knowledge gained, which can be directly communicated and objectively verified. This side of the human being is accessible to investigation by scientific disciplines, be it biology, physiology, biochemistry, psychology, cognitive science. As an empirical ego, man realizes himself in three modes of being, which build on each other and are interrelated.

"Mere" or *"biological existence"*: At this stage a human being lives out vital drives and bodily impulses. The intentions are directed to the nearest ends of life preservation. It is dominated by "the ruthless vital will to exist." (Ph III 108) Interests in power, prestige, and pleasure determine life. Absent from consciousness are processes of self-reflection. This mode of realization is similar to the stage of "aesthetic existence" in *Kierkegaard's* philosophy. This is not surprising, since Jaspers explicitly emphasized the dependence of his existential philosophy on *Kierkegaard*. In the epilogue written in 1955 on the genesis of the main work of existential philosophy, PHILOSOPHIE, he even declares that in this work he made *Kierkegaard's* concept of existence "his own" (Ph I, XX).

"Consciousness in general": This is the second human mode of being. Jaspers took over this term from *Kant* and means by it the activity of understanding and the categories of understanding which, as formal, universal structural elements, are (a priori) immanent in the human faculty of cognition. Whereas in mere existence one is directed towards the fulfilment of life-serving purposes, with this mode of being one realizes the capacity for clear and logical thinking. Consciousness in general

forms the necessary condition that human beings can mean something identically among themselves and accept it as generally valid.

The *"spirit"*: This is the third human mode of being that Jaspers distinguishes. By this he means ideas and contexts of meaning, which a human being can create for himself on the basis of the gift of reason. Ideas bring coherence "to the multiple finite purposes of my doing"; they bring "unity to the scatteredness of the knowable and the experienceable" (Ph II 53). As bearer of ideas, one arranges sense impressions and perceptions into comprehensive frames of orientation. As examples of this, Jaspers refers to the "idea of the university" in his philosophy of education, and to the "idea of democracy" in his political philosophy.

If the three modes of being or dimensions of realization mentioned so far constitute man as an empirically-rationally explorable living being. But every human being also possesses an existential level of being that is not empirically explorable. Jaspers often refers to this with the statement:

Man is fundamentally more than he can know of himself. (Einf. 50)

Only in the ascent into the form of life of "existence" or "actual selfhood" can a human being realize his highly individual, unjustifiable mode of being. Existential being is in principle not representable in empirical-rational categories and communicable as objective knowledge. For Jaspers, it means the "true" or "actual" human being.

3.3   Foundering as a Positive Impulse for Self-Realization

In Jaspers' reflections on the meaning of being human, foundering plays an essential role. Every human being is frequently confronted with this in the course of life. The elementary biological needs for unity, wholeness, security and safety can never be satisfied for any length of time, because man thus fails because of the antinomian structure of existence. When it comes to the unity and wholeness of oneself, an insurmountable obstacle is the split between body and mind. As a drive and instinct being, man can never become completely nature, because his spirit (ability to reflect) prevents him from doing so. But he is also unable to become completely spirit because his biological nature stands in his way. The contingency experiences of susceptibility to suffering and mortality are experienced as the foundering of longings for integrity and constant duration.

Many borderline experiences are associated with oppressive feelings of foundering. This also applies to the experience of the fundamental limits of the ability that distinguishes humanity from all other living beings: the ability to think and the capacity for self-reflection. As soon as it comes to questions of meaning in life, these cannot be answered by mere rationality of understanding. Even the scientifically active human being fails as soon as it comes to the answer to the question of what meaning science should have for the personal execution of life. The answer cannot be derived from scientific knowledge. For that it requires recourse to an value point of view. But such a point of view cannot be justified purely rationally, because it is ultimately based on a non-rational value decision.

As a "universal knower," man experiences an "absolute loneliness" because of the foundering of the capacity for reflection and cognition (Ph II 204). Jaspers writes about multiple ways of foundering as a consequence of the antinomian structure of "Dasein":

> *What* fails is not only *existence* as passing away, not only *cognition* as self-destruction in the attempt to comprehend being par excellence, not only *action* as the absence of a final purpose capable of enduring. In the borderline situations, it becomes apparent that everything positive to us is bound to the negative that belongs to it. (Ph III 220–221)

The significance of the thought motif of foundering in Jaspers' existential-philosophical and metaphysical thinking becomes apparent from the context in which this thought motif is central: foundering is experienced as soon as man comes up against the principal limit of the cognitive faculty in his orientation to the world, because he must experience that he can never recognize the world as a "whole".

Man also fails in the elucidation of his own selfhood. In self-reflection he has to experience that no complete recognition of his own being is attainable. For he possesses a "super-rational," transcendent dimension of being that always allows him to be "more than he can know of himself." As soon as the existentially elucidation self-reflection turns into practical existential fulfilment, he experiences "in his true, actual selfhood the most radical dependence" on "transcendence" (W 621) from which he experiences himself "as given". Thus his innermost striving for completely autonomous self-constitution and absolute freedom fails (Ph III 221).

That man also fails in all attempts to grasp transcendence intellectually, because it is in no way conceivable as an object, would suggest that foundering is always associated only with pessimistic or even nihilistic connotations.

However, the fact that Jaspers gives foundering also a positive accent results from the following consideration: The negativity of foundering is relativized by the antinomian structure of being, because one can always argue that in foundering only the negative side of the antinomy is experienced, but there is always a positive side as well. By "changing the consciousness of being" in foundering, impulses for overcoming the negative consequences can arise and open up new options for action and perspectives on life.

After every failure, no matter how depressing, there is in principle the possibility of a new beginning. Here an obvious parallel to *Hannah Arendt* becomes apparent, who in her theory of action gave central importance to the principle of "natality", "nativity" and "new beginnings". Human beings, because of the freedom they are given at birth, are in a position, by intervening in the "fabric of human affairs". They can always make a new beginning, from which new causal chains of action can also emerge in politics.[2]

---

[2] Cf. Hannah Arendt, *Vita activa oder vom tätigen Leben*, München 1996, 215–228.

Another reason for the positivity of foundering is its connection with Jaspers' ideal of meaning of life and true humanity.

A central assumption of the ideal of being human is Jaspers' philosophical-anthropological thesis that the human being only becomes "human" in the normative sense when he is able to realize his "possible existence". There exist two basic possibilities to realize this "higher" degree of self-realization and true humanity: the "right" overcoming of borderline situations as well as the existential communication with another human being.

3.3.1 Self-Realization by Overcoming Borderline Situations (Death, Suffering, Guilt, Struggle for Life)

Jaspers already develops the thought of the possibility of the "upswing" to true humanity in borderline situations in the PSYCHOLOGIE DER WELTANSCHAUUNGEN. In the Jaspers literature, this thought is also called "the philosophical original intention of the young Jaspers", which shaped his later works in many respects.[3] Other existential philosophers or existentialists have also emphasized that being human is necessarily always being in situations.[4] One always lives in situations in which one is already placed from birth (parents, gender, ethnicity, etc.). As soon as one changes a situation (friendships, living situation, professional situation, etc.), one enters into a new one.

The normal course of life in situations can suddenly be interrupted by the confrontation with a borderline situation. The term "Grenzsituation" or "borderline situation" is an original coinage of words by Jaspers, which has already entered everyday language. By this he means situations (in English translations also "limit situations", "ultimate situations") which all the usual and practiced procedures for coping with and changing situations experienced so far fail. The person who gets into a borderline situation and experiences it consciously fails with all rational strategies to solve critical situations and problems. This makes one aware of the insecurity, questionability and finiteness of life.

> The acting human being ... stands beyond all individual situations in certain decisive essential situations which are ... inevitably given with being human ... These situations, which are felt, experienced, thought everywhere at the borders of our existence, we therefore call 'borderline situations'. What they have in common is that ... there is *nothing fixed*, no undoubted absolute, no hold that would withstand any experience and any thinking. Everything flows, is in restless movement of being questioned, everything is relative, finite, split into opposites, never the whole, the absolute, the essential. (PW 229)

---

[3] Cf. Edwin Latzel, Die Erhellung der Grenzsituation. In: Paul A. Schilpp (ed.), *Karl Jaspers*, Stuttgart 1957, 169.

[4] Cf. Jean Paul Sartre, *Sein und Nichtsein. Versuch einer ontologischen Phänomenologie*, Hamburg 1962, 610–695.

> Borderline situations are … like a wall against which we bump, against which we founder.. They cannot be changed by anything, but only brought to clarity, without being able to explain and derive them from another. (Ph II 203)

In the PSYCHOLOGIE DER WELTANSCHAUUNGEN, the antinomian structure of existence and suffering are called as general borderline situations, and struggle, death, contingency and guilt as particular borderline situations. In the main work of philosophy of existence, PHILOSOPHIE, somewhat differently: the borderline situation of the historical determinacy of existence, as well as the individual borderline situations: Death, suffering, struggle and guilt, and finally that borderline situation which Jaspers here no longer calls the borderline situation of the antinomian structure of Dasein, but "the borderline situation of the questionability of all being and of the historicity of the real in general".

With "historicity" Jaspers takes up a concept that has a significant place in the hermeneutic discussion of the method of understanding in the humanities and cultural studies. In an existential philosophical understanding, it serves to denote a central moment of the structure of subjectivity (existence, selfhood, actual Dasein) in connection with the inescapable situationality of the human being. Jaspers also associates "historicity" with openness, freedom, self-determination, unconditionality of action, concreteness, subjectivity, individuality, spontaneity. Thus historicity becomes the opposite of closedness, abstractness, dogmatism, perfectionism, determinism, collectivism and hostility to communication. Jaspers illustrates this opposition by contrasting "historicity" and "catholicity."

> The historicity of man stands in communication from existence to existence, in which what actually is only becomes. Catholicity has created a community in which only that which is objectively identical for all is communicated and believed in, with the urge for the recurring function of the same. Instead of the upwardly drifting battle of spirits, there is command and obedience, there is communication of truth possession, which the other only has to accept …. (W 843)

Experiencing borderline situations can cause people to engage in intensive processes of self-reflection. In doing so, he becomes aware of his own non-objectifiable dimension of inwardness, personal existence and individual freedom. From this dimension he is able to withstand all shocks. One can thereby gain a final foothold and a new "power of life" from which new "attitudes towards life" (PW 262) are developed for overcoming the respective borderline situation and a new self-assessment and worldview are achieved.

> To borderline situations, therefore, we respond meaningfully not by plan and calculation in order to overcome them, but by an entirely different activity, the becoming of the existence possible in us; we become ourselves by entering the borderline situation with our eyes open … Experiencing borderline situations and existing are the same thing. (Ph II 204)

In the description of borderline situations, the following is typical of Jaspers' mode of presentation: he first names inauthentic attitudes that lead away from true selfhood and then contrasts these with preferable authentic attitudes that enable the positive coping with borderline situations. Undoubtedly, experiences from Jaspers' psychiatric work played an important role in this procedure.

In relation to the *borderline situation* of *death*, be it the knowledge of one's own imminent death or the experience of the death of a close person, the following are named as refusable attitudes: nihilistic despair, ecstatic lust for life, isolation from emotional shocks. As preferable attitudes are considered: "inner appropriation" of death and bravery (Ph II 225).

As far as the *borderline situation of struggle* is concerned, Jaspers emphasizes, in contrast to the cunning and deceitful and often violent struggle for the fulfillment of narrow-minded, vital interests of existence, the "loving struggle" for openness towards oneself and towards others.

In the *borderline situation of suffering* it is important not to suppress the experience of suffering or to lapse into lethargic passivity, but to integrate it actively into the further course of life through inner appropriation.

For the *borderline situation of guilt,* repression of guilt and superficial self-justification are rejected and personal readiness to take responsibility is urged.

The *borderline situation of the questionability of existence* should not be met by disguising experienced contradictions through the construction of harmonizing world-views. Rather, it is necessary to internalize a basic attitude from which the entire contradictoriness of life is accepted.

3.3.2   Self-Realization in Interpersonal Communication

The idea of communication is one of the central motifs in Jaspers' philosophy.[5] It has as its focus the basic anthropological fact that man is by nature a social or communicative being and that the realization of being human necessarily presupposes communication with other people. Therefore, it seems only consistent when Jaspers also connects specific forms of interpersonal communication with the aforementioned dimensions of human self-realization.

"*Mere existence*" is determined by communication in "primitive communality" (Ph II 54–56). This is about the satisfaction of vital drives and egoistic life impulses. Other people are instrumentalized for the sake of fulfilling such drives. As communication partners they are arbitrarily exchangeable and replaceable. In mere means-purpose relationships, anyone who contributes to the achievement of the desired vital goal is accepted.

To "*consciousness in general*" Jaspers assigns communication in "objective purposefulness and rationality". The gift of understanding makes it possible to communicate with other people on the basis of generally valid, logical rules and categories of thought and to reach agreement in the assessment of facts. Scientific discussion could be seen as a prototype of such form of communication. But also on this level the communication partners are exchangeable. They can be replaced by

---

[5] Cf. Hans Saner, *Karl Jaspers*, Reinbek 2005, 101; Jürgen Habermas, *Philosophisch-politische Profile*, Frankfurt 1981, 87.

others who judge according to the same criteria of rationality, but who have a higher capacity for reflection.

In the dimension of *"spirit"* or reason, communication takes place in "idea-determined spirituality of content". This form of communication is "substantial" for Jaspers, because mutual understanding is given. This is based on the common sharing of meaning and ideas. Such a communicative relationship, however, still conveys an insufficiency, because it does not yet entail the realization of true selfhood. This is realized only in existential communication with a fellow human being.

Here, two communication partners realize themselves as independent and unrepresentable subjects who are not interchangeable in the common relationship. Such relationships of an intimate character can be: love relationships, friendship relationships, parent-child relationships, a happy relationship between spouses. Whether such a relationship could also exist in a doctor-patient relationship is at least hinted at by Jaspers as an idea (AZ 15).

3.4   The Human Being in Relation to the Encompassing, Transcendent Being

That for Jaspers true humanity necessarily possesses a metaphysical dimension becomes clear from his understanding of transcendence and from the doctrine of the encompassing. From his point of view, man always experiences a reference to transcendence in the realization of individual existence. Similarly to *Kierkegaard*, he once formulated:

> *Existence* is the selfhood that relates to itself and therein to transcendence, through which it knows itself to be given, and on which it is founded. (E 113)

The relationship to transcendence is what Jaspers calls "philosophical faith" in explicit contrast to confessional, religious faith.

The "encompassing" forms the metaphysical frame of reference of Jaspers' conception of being human:

> That which cannot be transcended, that which cannot be grasped even as such, that out of which we are and which we therefore never survey, that which is always still more comprehensive, no matter how comprehensively we determine our object to be known, we call the encompassing. (W 26)[6]

Jaspers developed the reference to an encompassing, transcendent being in a differentiated way in the Periechontology (doctrine of being) by distinguishing different modes of the encompassing.

What was presented as modes of being or realization of dimensions of man from the existential philosophical considerations (mere existence, consciousness in

---

[6]Cf. Gerhard Knauss, Der Begriff des Umgreifenden in Jaspers' Philosophie. In: Paul A. Schilpp (ed.), *Karl Jaspers*, Stuttgart 1957, 130–163.

general, spirit, existence), is reinterpreted as *a priori* frames of reference or non-representational, open "spaces", "horizons", "origins" or "conditions of possibilities". In these, everything that exists can come into appearance and the ideal of being human can be realized in all its possible manifestations. But these transcendental conditions of all being human also refer to a final, no longer conceivable dimension of being:

> But we call transcendence in the proper sense only the encompassing par excellence, the encompassing of all that is encompassed. It is of an original single content. It is the transcendence of transcendences, as opposed to the general transcendence that belongs to every mode of grasping. (W 109)

3.5   Being Human Through Reason

In Jaspers' main work in the philosophy of existence, PHILOSOPHIE, reason does not yet have a systematic function. It only acquires such a function in the writings VERNUNFT UND EXISTENZ from 1935 and VON DER WAHRHEIT from 1948. It should be noted, however, that Jaspers' concept of reason, which he uses in the works after the existential-philosophical period, is ambiguous. Some accents of meaning can be clarified if one asks about tasks that Jaspers assigns to reason. As has already been indicated, being human represents for Jaspers a dynamic process of becoming without an end result. In this respect, reason is "a constant demand and movement" or a "boundless driving forward" (VE 38).

The individual, guided by reason, rejects illusions of unity, wholeness, and totality by relativizing them and exposing them as illusions. Reason must expose the feigned unity and totality of the scientific worldview as "science superstition" (Ph I 123, 140, 142–143).[7] Reason emphasizes the multiplicity of possibilities of being and calls into consciousness the antinomian basic structure of all being. A special function of reason is to foster in each individual the readiness to communicate.

---

[7] Cf. also: Karl Jaspers, Wahrheit und Wissenschaft. In: ders, *Philosophische Aufsätze,* Frankfurt 1967, 62–77.

Liberal Ethos of Humanity, Science and Education

4.1   Was Jaspers a Moralist of the Twentieth Century?

The term "moralist" is used in a broad sense in cultural and intellectual history; it is by no means limited to philosophy. In the history of literature, authors of socially critical utopias are referred to as "moralists" because they confront political and social reality with fictional, utopian concepts of society with a critical intention. Examples of this in the early modern period are *Thomas More* with the writing UTOPIA (1516), *Tomaso Campanella* with the book on the SUNSHINE STATE (1602), or *Francis Bacon* with NOVA ATLANTIS (1643). *Jonathan Swift*'s GULLIVER'S TRAVELS (1726), often misunderstood as a children's book, also belongs to the category of literature that authors have used to criticize society with the help of utopian writings for moral purposes. The fact that different types of utopias need to be distinguished in this context has been emphasized in the specialist discussion on the subject of utopia.[1]

In eighteenth-century France, the word "moralist" was used to describe, among others, philosophers who collaborated in French Enlightenment philosophy on the huge project of the famous French ENCYCLOPÄDIE (Encyclopédie ou dictionnaire raisonné des sciences, des arts et des métiers) between 1751 and 1784. The authors include *Denis Diderot, Jean-Baptist D'Alembert, Le Chevalier de Jaucourt* and also *François Marie Voltaire*. The aim of these philosophers was to transmit the knowledge of the time to a broad public by a popular encyclopedia. They were convinced that morally valuable action would necessarily result from reason alone, when purified from prejudice by knowledge. From the perspective of modern ethical discussion, the French Enlightenment philosophers would be called "cognitivists". They assumed a close connection between rational knowledge on the one hand and moral action on the other. In this respect Jaspers differs from the French moralists of the eighteenth century. He shares with them neither the unconditional trust in the

---

[1] Cf. Richard Saage, *Politische Utopien der Neuzeit*, Darmstadt 1991.

K. Salamun, *Karl Jaspers*, https://doi.org/10.1007/978-3-476-05896-6_4

moral-positive function of reason nor the uncritical appreciation of the rational, scientific style of thinking.

One striking commonality between Jaspers and the French Enlightenment philosophers, however, is the following: Like the French moralists, Jaspers was deeply imbued with an Enlightenment ethos. He wanted to pass on his philosophical thoughts and humane value ideas to as many people as possible. These were to be induced to self-reflection processes about their own possible existence and the ability of their reason. As already mentioned in the biographical section, Jaspers also wanted to make his philosophy known to a broad public through radio and television. That he was a moralist is confirmed last but not least by his successor in Heidelberg, *Hans Georg Gadamer.* He states:

> Jaspers was also, in his engagement with the tradition of philosophy, the great moralist he became in his Basel decades as a political writer. It is strange enough that in our country the figure of the moralist is so little known and appreciated in its own legitimacy. Word and thing come from the French cultural world, and the great examples of a Montaigne or La Rochefoucauld are unknown in the German world of to-day. Schopenhauer and Nietzsche, who saw in them their great model, remained outsiders to the school tradition. It is the distinction of Karl Jaspers that he was in one a superior philosophical teacher and a moralist.[2]

For the German political philosopher *Hermann Lübbe,* too, Jaspers was a moralist, at least as far as his political philosophy is concerned.[3] As such, Jaspers was at the same time a humanist who, as a philosopher and political thinker, strove for the widest possible dissemination of humane values and liberal-democratic ideas.

4.2   On the Appellative-Ethical Intention of Philosophizing

Jaspers did not want to be an ethicist or moral philosopher who develops an explicit ethics or doctrine of morality. He rejected out of hand efforts to develop a systematic doctrine of morality or a "system" of moral values. In none of his works is there any discussion of hierarchies of values or ethical generalization principles. Also absent from his philosophy are postulates regarding a moral highest value and reflections on how one might justify such a value.

If one asks why Jaspers did not want to develop ethics, one can cite influences from *Max Weber, Kierkegaard,* and *Nietzsche. Weber,* in discussions of the relationship between social scientific knowledge and ultimate axioms of value,

---

[2] Hans-Georg Gadamer, Philosophische Begegnungen. In: ders, Hermeneutik im Rückblick. In: ders, *Gesammelte Werke, 10th vol.* Tübingen 1995, 399.

[3] Hermann Lübbe, Die Masse, der Nationalsozialismus und die Atombombe, Karl Jaspers als politischer Moralist. In: Reinhard Schulz, Giandomenico Bonanni et al. (eds.), *"Wahrheit ist, was uns verbindet" Karl Jaspers' Kunst zu philosophieren,* Göttingen 2009, 391–410.

argued that the ultimate axioms of value and ideals that guide our actions are subjective beliefs. As such, they defy rational justification and discussion.[4]

Another reason for the aversion to ethics may be the influence that *Nietzsche* and *Kierkegaard* exerted on Jaspers with their criticism of rationalism. Both devalued the intellect (the ratio) and held against it the pulsating life and an irrational, subjective existence as the highest value. This influence is evident in Jaspers' aversion to rational systems. Such systems could all too easily become rigid schemata that decisively limit the diversity of possible perceptual phenomena, life impulses, and worldview value points. *Nietzsche* expressed system aversion very drastically when he wrote in Aphorism 26th of GÖTZEN-DÄMMERUNG (1889):

I distrust all systematics and avoid them. The will to system is a lack of righteousness.[5]

Here *Nietzsche* rejects the will to system-building by invoking a moral category, namely the principle of righteousness. Weber also emphatically emphasizes this principle, albeit under a different name, namely "intellectual honesty".

This principle is also central to Jaspers' philosophy. It is an essential component of the liberal ethos of humanity, which can be seen as the fundamental, moral framework of Jaspers' entire thought. This ethos is already expressed in the early book PSYCHOLOGIE DER WELTANSCHAUUNGEN in its critique of the rational housings of worldviews. The fixation on worldviews, when they appear as ethical systems, substantially limits individual decision-making in morally relevant situations (cf. PW 304–305). Such systems, in Jaspers' view, not only present certain values as correct and generally binding, but also make their acceptance obligatory. Thus, the individual value decision is suggestively steered in a very specific direction. It no longer takes place autonomously or "necessarily" out of self-determining subjectivity.

Now it is precisely the central task of philosophy, as Jaspers understands it, to advocate individual freedom of choice and the greatest possible openness to various possibilities of individual self-realization. Philosophy must ensure that the dynamic processes and principles of being human, such as critical self-reflection, self-responsible self-selection, as well as unconditional, autonomous value-decision out of existential freedom, must not be abandoned at the expense of self-satisfied security and self-assurance, as suggested by rational worldviews and ethical systems.

It is part of the methodological peculiarity of Jaspers' philosophy - I refer mainly to the existential philosophical period - that he does not want to convey his liberal ethos of humanity in a direct way through convincing justificatory arguments for certain moral principles and through explicit ethical postulates. Rather, his methodological intention is to appeal indirectly to each individual to join in the thought processes of his philosophizing and to appropriate this ethos himself in a process of "inner action." The point of this method, as the Swiss jaspers-researcher *Anton*

---

[4]Cf. Max Weber, Wissenschaft als Beruf. In: ders, *Gesammelte Aufsätze zur Wissenschaftslehre*, 3. erw. Und verb. ed. Tübingen 1993, 603–609.

[5]Friedrich Nietzsche, Götzendämmerung. In: ders, *Sämtliche Werke. Kritische Studienausgabe*, vol. 6, München 1988, 63.

Hügli rightly points out, is not merely to present facts, but to "convey the attitude of the communicator toward the facts."[6] With the indirect method of communication, Jaspers invokes not only *Kierkegaard* as a model, but also *Socrates*. An ambivalent quasi-definition of Jaspers about this method, however, comes close to mysticism:

> Indirect communication means that with the strongest urge for clarity and all searching for forms and formulas, no expression is sufficient and man becomes aware of this, means the attitude that everything communicated that is directly there, sayable, is ultimately the unessential, but at the same time indirectly the bearer of the essential. (PW 378)

4.3   Are Humane Value Positions Irrational from Jaspers' Point of View?

In the existential philosophical phase of his thought, Jaspers created the impression that value decisions are based only on irrational, subjective acts of faith. This impression comes about through methodological statements that in existential philosophizing the "representationality" of statements must be "transcended". All philosophical statements are to be brought into "suspension" in their contents of meaning. Thus, in the concluding section of VERNUNFT UND EXISTENZ, it is required to use "negative, circular, and dialectical statements" so that "what is said as the supposed knowledge of a certain thing cancels itself out again." (VE 74).

Does this confirm the criticism of the American Jaspers interpreter *William Earle* that Jaspers' philosophical appeals ultimately call for "incomprehensible tasks" if the meaning content of his statements has to be suspended or transcended again?[7] This problem was recognized early in the Jaspers-discussion by the German philosopher *Otto Friedrich Bollnow*, who meant in reference to Jaspers' existential philosophy:

> At the moment when philosophy withdraws from any possibility of fixing it to certain opinions of content, when it takes itself only as an appealing thinking, it gives away the possibility of a fruitful discussion at all. ... With the retreat to the non-fixability of each individual statement a ... position is taken that with it at the same time every possibility of a real discussion, indeed the possibility of a meaningful discussion at all is taken away.[8]

The criticism of an understanding of philosophy that wants philosophical statements to be understood merely as "pointers" or "guides" to something non-representational, unspeakable, essential, is certainly justified. From such a point of view, every substantive statement about humane values can be countered with the

---

[6] Anton Hügli, Indirekte Kommunikation. Inwiefern es Grenzen der Mitteilung gibt. In: ders., *Von der Schwierigkeit vernünftig zu sein*, Basel 2016, 181.

[7] Cf. William A. Earle, Die Anthropologie in Jaspers' Philosophie. In: Paul A. Schilpp (ed.), *Karl Jaspers*, Stuttgart 1957, 529.

[8] Otto Friedrich Bollnow, Existenzerhellung und philosophische Anthropologie. Versuch einer Auseinandersetzung mit Karl Jaspers. In: Hans Saner (ed.), *Karl Jaspers in der Diskussion*, München 1973, 211.

argument that it does not actually meet what is meant, because this cannot be expressed at all in terms of content.[9]

Is Jaspers an irrationalist with regard to the articulation of humane value positions? If so, he would be taking a similar standpoint that has been taken in positions of early philosophical neopositivism. His contemporary *Ludwig Wittgenstein*, in his book TRACTATUS LOGICO-PHILOSOPHICUS, held that there could be "no propositions of ethics" because what they are about "cannot be expressed at all."[10]

The ambivalent attitude that Jaspers took in the discussion of values during his existential philosophical phase is also shown by the following circumstance: on the one hand, he warns against the rationalization of the existential dimension of being human and denies the possibility of objectification of it from the outset. On the other hand, however, he suggests the appropriation of value attitudes that are constitutive of his liberal ethos of humanity. This ambivalent basic attitude makes it difficult to classify Jaspers' ethos of humanity in one of the usual positions of moral philosophy. If value standpoints are irrational for him, then he would withdraw them from rational discussion and make value decisions to acts of will that cannot be rationally grasped. He would thereby not only abandon the rational justification of his humane value ideas, but also the possibility of a rational criticism of inhumane value decisions.

Important questions to ask in relation to Jaspers' moral philosophical standpoint, therefore, are as follows:

How does Jaspers see the relationship between rational knowledge and subjective value decision, between factual knowledge and the orientation towards humane values (virtues) in morally relevant decision and action situations?

Does the decision to existentially choose of oneself always already include the value attitudes as necessary conditions for the possibility of existential self-realization?

Does the unconditionality of self-selection preclude any fact-based, rational consideration of the possible implications and consequences of orienting oneself to these virtues?

Only after Jaspers has said goodbye to dubious methodological presuppositions of his existential philosophy ("transcending" philosophizing, philosophizing "in abeyance", "indirect communication", "negative" and "dialectical statements" "cancelling out" the cognitive content of statements, etc.) and has developed a philosophy of reason, these questions can be answered. Both in the book DIE ATOMBOMBE UND DIE ZUKUNFT DES MENSCHEN and in the later writing and lecture collection KLEINE SCHULE DES PHILOSOPHISCHEN DENKENS (1965) there are clear statements on this problem. There, the close link between rational cognition and value decision is pointed out. Thus it is said in DIE ATOMBOMBE UND DIE ZUKUNFT DES MENSCHEN:

---

[9] Cf. my critique in: Kurt Salamun, *Karl Jaspers*, Würzburg 2006, 30.

[10] Cf. Ludwig Wittgenstein, *Tractatus logico-philosophicus*. In: ders, *Werkausgabe Vol. I*, Frankfurt 1984, 83.

For reason requires knowledge of the mind: one must know what is in order to know what one wants. (AZM 254)

In the section "Cognition and Value Judgment" in the KLEINE SCHULE DES PHI-LOSOPHISCHEN DENKENS, the passage is found:

No binding norms can be derived from facts … Science cannot show me the meaning of life, but it can develop for me the meaning of what I want and thereby perhaps change the goal of the will itself. (KlSch 96)

This makes clear how far Jaspers has turned away from the irrational components of his existential philosophy in his late philosophy. To be sure, he still does not advocate a consistently rationalist moral philosophy. But he now explicitly emphasizes that empirical-rational, factual knowledge has a relevant significance for the choice of will goals and value decisions.

Thus he can be called a representative of a moderate non-cognitivist standpoint in questions of value. He thus does justice to the following two indisputable facts that speak against radical non-rationalism (non-cognitivism) in questions of value:

1. Value positions and value decisions are usually also based on rational situation interpretations and a certain amount of factual knowledge. When situation interpretations are changed by falsification of the factual knowledge on which the respective situation interpretation is based, will goals and value standpoints often change as well, although this need not of course be the case in a compelling and logically necessary manner.
2. A high degree of factual knowledge is not an obstacle to unreserved and unqualified commitment to a value standpoint. This is demonstrated by the consideration that it is only through knowledge of the implications and consequences associated with a value standpoint that the responsibility dimension of a value decision comes fully into focus. One could also say that relevant factual knowledge about implications and possible consequences of value standpoints and value decisions form the prerequisite for making a truly autonomous, self-responsible and unconditional decision for a volitional goal or value standpoint in Jaspers' sense.

In the Jaspers-discussion there are several attempts to examine the complete work with regard to ethical statements and humane values and to prove the influence of other thinkers.

Thus, *Hannah Arendt* has particularly emphasized the influence of *Kant*'s ethics of duty.[11] One finds this influence in sentences in which *Kant's* categorical imperative is varied. Thus it is said in the second volume of PHILOSOPHIE:

What I do should be such that I can want the world in general to be such that it should happen everywhere. (Ph II, 269)

---

[11] Hannah Arendt, *Karl Jaspers. Wahrheit, Freiheit und Friede*, München 1958, 32–33.

Helmut Fahrenbach refers to the *Kierkegaard* influence by locating ethical components of Jaspers' existential philosophy in an "existential-dialectical ethics". *Fahrenbach* sees the central aspect of the "existential-dialectical interpretation of the ethical" in the fact that this

> "made visible *as a* determination of existence and an understanding of existence, and the subjective problem of ethical existence is brought into focus."[12]

The fact that *Franz Peter Burkard* interprets central concepts of Jaspers' existential philosophy, such as "being able to be oneself", "wanting to be oneself", "inner action", "unconditional will to choose oneself", "upsurge of being oneself", in the sense of an ethics of striving, is also one of the interesting interpretative hypotheses of the humane, moral philosophical implications in Jaspers.[13]

Last but not least, *Hans Saner* also made an important contribution to the discussion. He drew attention to the fact that in Jaspers one is confronted "with two fundamentally different forms of ethics", namely "with the contemplative reflection of ethics as a discipline in a few passages of the work and with … an indirect appellative ethos throughout the work."[14]

4.4   Humane Values of the Liberal Ethos of Humanity

The most important humane value attitudes that Jaspers wants to convey can be reconstructed in his philosophy from passages on borderline situations, existence, freedom, communication, reason and philosophical faith. One could also interpret the value attitudes referred to there as virtues, if one accepts the following definition by *Otfried Höffe:* Virtues are "ideals of education and (self-)education to a humanly excellent personality."[15]

Fahrenbach's definition in an article on "Existential Dialectical Ethics" also captures what is meant here:

---

[12] Helmut Fahrenbach, Existenzdialektische Ethik. In: Annemarie Pieper (ed.), *Geschichte der neueren Ethik,* Tübingen, Basel 1992, 274.

[13] Cf. Franz P. Burkard, Existenzphilosophie und Strebensethik. In: *Jb. der Österreichischen Karl-Jaspers-Gesellschaft,* vol. 12 (1999), 29–41; Franz P. Burkard, *Ethische Existenz bei Karl Jaspers,* Würzburg 1982.

[14] Hans Saner, Zum systematischen Ort der ethischen Reflexion im Denken von Karl Jaspers. In: *Jb. der Österreichischen Karl-Jaspers-Gesellschaft,* vol. 12 (1999), 10–11; cf. also: Tsuyoshi Nakayama, Die Wende des ethischen Denkmotivs bei Karl Jaspers von der "Ethik der Existenz" zur "Ethik der Vernunft". In: *Jb. der Österreichischen Karl-Jaspers-Gesellschaft,* vol. 28 (2015), 63–77.

[15] Cf. Otfried Höffe, Tugend. In: ders, *Lexikon der Ethik,* München 6th ed. 2002, 267.

Virtues are basic attitudes of behavior and character traits to which a person must personally develop ... in order to arrive at a situation-related ethically responsible behavior and
'action' in the circumstances of life.[16]

Virtues or humane values must not be understood as rigidly fixed, general norms for
morally correct decisions and actions in certain types of situations. They must
always be internalized anew in subjective processes of appropriation, i.e. in processes of "inner action". Only in this way they can become effective as unconditional moral decisions of individuals in situations demanding moral actions.

4.4.1 Humane Values in Coping with Borderline Situations

As already explained, Jaspers does not see the experience of borderline situations
and the associated foundering only negatively. Through foundering one can also be
referred to one's own individuality and existential freedom. In PHILOSOPHIE, several
value attitudes are mentioned that are connected with the positive coping with borderline situations.

In view of the *borderline situation of death* there is talk of "dignity" and "serenity in the knowledge of the end", of "illusionlessness" and bravery. The latter is also
expressed in the renunciation of the hope that death merely means the transition to
another life.

Bravery in the face of death as the end of everything that is really visible and rememberable
to me is reduced to a minimum when, through sensual ideas of the afterlife, death is
annulled as a limit and made into a mere transition between forms of existence. It has lost
the horror of non-being. It ceases to be true dying. (Ph II, 225)

The illusionless attitude towards death, which for Jaspers corresponds to the dignity
of being human, does justice to the principle of intellectual honesty that he so highly
esteems. This virtue is not expressed, as he explicitly emphasizes, in the resigned or
cynical "making meaningless" of all that has been done in life. Rather, it is based on
reflection on "what remains *essential* in *the face of death.*" (Ph II 223) In this context, the virtue of earnestness or seriousness of life is also emphasized.

For the *borderline situation* of *guilt,* the virtue of taking on personal responsibility is central. This is not only about the willingness to take responsibility for negative consequences of intended actions. The negative consequences of non-intended,
spontaneous actions and of deliberate non-action in decision-making situations
must also be included. That Jaspers has always argued for individual responsibility
as opposed to anonymizing group responsibility follows from his understanding of
existence and freedom. Only through the willingness to attribute responsibility individually and to have it attributed to oneself, could the evasion of responsibility be
counteracted. Jaspers had already critically focused on both the appeal to

---

[16] Helmut Fahrenbach, Existenzdialektische Ethik. In: Annemarie Pieper (ed.), *Geschichte der
neueren Ethik,* vol. 1, Tübingen, Basel 1992, 274.

irresistible, technical-rational constraints and the manifold tendencies to anonymize responsibility in the complicated decision-making processes of democratic mass societies.

On the scope and various aspects of the concept of responsibility and guilt as developed by Jaspers in his book DIE SCHULDFRAGE, *Dominic Kaegi* has presented a differentiating investigation in an article entitled "What is Metaphysical Guilt?".[17]

For the *borderline situation of suffering*, as actual value attitudes are emphasized: to fight suffering as far as possible and, where this is no longer possible, to bear it bravely in inner appropriation (cf. Ph II, 230–233). In spite of experiences of suffering, however burdensome, one must always strive for positive possibilities of experience and not isolate oneself against them.

As far as the *borderline situation of struggle* is concerned, the "loving struggle" is recommended as a positive value attitude.

For the *borderline situation of the questionability of Dasein* or the "antinomian basic structure of all Dasein", Jaspers pleads for a humane basic attitude, from which one is prepared to understand "the brokenness, dividedness and contradictoriness" of Dasein as an "unceasing demand to become different" (cf. Ph II 253). One can also understand the basic humane attitude in this borderline situation as a fundamental confidence in life and as a "trust in being". In VON DER WAHRHEIT Jaspers calls it philosophical faith.

4.4.2 Humane Values for the Success of Interpersonal Communication

A prerequisite for successful communication is that two communication partners are able *to bear loneliness* (cf. Ph II 61–63). For a fulfilling relationship between two persons, the moment of "listening into oneself" and autonomous self-contemplation is needed. The phenomenon of inwardness that is at stake here must not be confused with "mere sociological isolation". It refers to moments of "pausing" from external activities in order to gain space for personal contemplation and creative meditation. Jaspers considers such moments especially important in light of tendencies toward the leveling and depersonalization of individuals. One might say that Jaspers encourages phases of life in which one gives priority to a meditative-creative solitude over hectic external activities.

As a further virtue in Jaspers' ideal of communication, he mentions the *readiness for unconditional, mutual openness* (cf. Ph II 64–65). He advocates unconditionally communicating one's own views and convictions to the relational partner without "masks" and allowing them to be questioned. This virtue can be described as the risk of exposing oneself as a whole personality to critical scrutiny by the relationship partner without camouflaging reassurance and disguising manoeuvres.

---

[17]Cf. Dominic Kaegi, Was ist metaphysische Schuld? In: *Jb. der Österreichischen Karl-Jaspers-Gesellschaft,* Vol. 14 (2001), 9–39.

The postulate of reciprocity and the virtue of *truthfulness* ensure that one communication partner does not instrumentalize the other for egoistic goals and does not take off his own "masks".

This is directly related to the postulate of non-egoistic commitment to the other(s). Jaspers speaks of the loving, *solidary struggle* on the existential level. This struggle implies the recognition of the *principle equality* of the communication partner.

> It is rather an expression of existential consciousness … that I … step on the same level with everyone, insofar as I seek communication, may he otherwise be far above me or below me in comparable matters; for in everyone, as in me, I presuppose origin and properness. (Ph II 85)

Jaspers' ideal of interpersonal communication is thus connected with the following humane value attitudes: The courage for meditative-creative solitude and autonomous, not externally determined self-reflection; the will to openness as the willingness to encounter other people without camouflaging reassurances and to allow one's own views and convictions to be questioned without reservation; the readiness for a non-egoistic commitment to others; the readiness to recognize other people in the possibility of their self-realization as equal in principle, despite their differences in comparable external matters, such as gender, social status, financial circumstances, level of education, ethnic origin, etc.

4.4.3   Humane Values in the Context of Reason

The value attitudes reconstructed so far from Jaspers' existential philosophy also play a central role in the later philosophy of reason and political philosophy. This can be shown by analyzing the understanding of reason in Periechontology (doctrine of encompassing being) in more detail. In VON DER WAHRHEIT, reason is given the function of creating a balance between the individual modes of being and of preventing one of them from becoming absolute and dominant. Through reason, untrue ideas of unity and totality are to be relativized. A particularly important task of reason, as will be shown here later, is to promote communication. In the remarks on the relationship between reason and interpersonal communication, Jaspers explicitly refers to basic human values by speaking of loyalty, reliability, trust, solidarity, the "melting down of self-will", as it is metaphorically called (cf. AZM 301).

4.4.4   Humane Values for Political Action

In his political phase of thought after 1945, Jaspers transferred the early existential-philosophical concept of the borderline situation onto the political world situation. He speaks of a "universal borderline situation" with which the whole of humanity is confronted. Through the modern development of technology, two dangers have arisen that have never existed before in the history of mankind: the danger of the collective self-extermination of mankind through the hydrogen bomb, as well as the danger of the establishment of a worldwide totalitarian government due to the development of new techniques for mass communication and mass control. From today's perspective, Jaspers would certainly also include the danger of a worldwide climate collapse and the danger of the abolition of the hitherto human being through the misuse of genetic manipulation among the universal borderline situations.

In view of this situation endangering the whole of humanity, reason became for Jaspers the instance that should bring about a "moral conversion" or, as he says in DIE ATOMBOMBE UND DIE ZUKUNFT DES MENSCHEN, the radical change of the "moral-political way of thinking" (cf. AZM 321–338). Reason is an essential component of that dimension of the "supra-political" from which the "old politics" in its fixation on power and closedminded interests had to be reshaped. The fact that in connection with the concept of the super-political the soldierly virtue of the courage to make sacrifices is also particularly emphasized, this may perhaps seem strange from today's perspective.[18]

The values listed here could also be summarized in the following general, humane principles: the principle of intellectual honesty, the principle of individual freedom, solidarity, equal recognition in partnership, openness and tolerance, the principle of human commitment, and the principle of personal responsibility. As far as the principle of individual freedom is concerned, Jaspers linked it in the political writings with the principle of political freedom and drew attention to interrelations between the freedom of individuals and the political freedom of all in a social system.

The basic values of Jaspers' liberal ethos of humanity could be supplemented by the following catalogue of values: the acceptance and respect of the uniqueness, indefensibility and irreplaceability of each human being; the value of unconstrained, autonomous self-determination and individual freedom; the courage for independent self-reflection; methodical individualism, from which the explanation of social and political phenomena by collective entities and holistic ideas such as state, class, ethnic tribe etc., is rejected in principle; individual values such as loyalty, trust, openness, readiness to communicate, etc.; the value of the single individual as a human being; individual values such as loyalty, trust, openness, willingness to communicate.

As far as the dissemination of these values is concerned, Jaspers relies on the role of reasonable individuals. These individuals should exemplify these values and contribute to their dissemination, both in the private sphere and in public. Among such individuals, he counts politicians, teachers and educators as role models. The university, too, must contribute to the dissemination of humane basic values by imparting value-oriented education.

---

[18]Cf. Reiner Wiehl, Jaspers' Bestimmung des Überpolitischen. In: Reiner Wiehl, Dominic Kaegi (Hg.), *Karl Jaspers - Philosophie und Politik*, Heidelberg 1999, 91–96.

4.5   The Limits of the Humane Values of Openness and Tolerance

Jaspers' philosophy has often been characterized as an expression of a way of thinking that contains a principled appeal to openness and tolerance. But this raises the following question: Does Jaspers emphasize these two principles so strongly that limits to openness and tolerance are lost from view? The fundamental appeal to openness is already to be found in that phase of thought in which Jaspers did not yet see himself as a philosopher at all. Already during his work as a psychologist, the principle of openness emerges in the following idea: the human worldview must not be fixed in a closed rationalistic worldview, but must always remain open (PW 281).

That Jaspers was strongly influenced by *Kierkegaard* in his early thinking in discussing the dichotomy of openness and closedness can be seen in many passages of PSYCHOLOGIE DER WELTANSCHAUUNGEN. After all, *Kierkegaard* was considered by him at the time to be the "greatest psychologist of worldviews." (PW 13) Kierkegaard had recognized the dialectical tension between "closedness" and "openness" in the basic existential structure of the human being and had come to the insight that the "process of becoming open is identical with becoming oneself" and that "becoming open means freedom", while "enclosing oneself means bondage" (cf. PW 221).

In PHILOSOPHIE, the ideal of openness plays an important role because it represents a constitutive moment of existential elucidation. ("Existenzerhellung,"). By analogy with *Kierkegaard's* conception of "subjective reflection,"[19] this means a process of engaged self-reflection and "becoming open to oneself." Jaspers also calls it the process of permanent "self-communication" as distinct from mere "self-study" (Ph II 39).

As far as the realization of existence itself is concerned, the principle of openness is of great importance both for becoming existence in borderline situations and in interpersonal communication. Already the awareness of a situation as a borderline situation presupposes a risk of openness. Security and safety, which have been gained by holding on to hitherto successful, rational problem-solving procedures, have to be surrendered (cf. Ph II 204). The "inner appropriation" of the respective borderline situation and a genuine acceptance of the personal fate founded in it can only come about through a "becoming open to oneself". Thereby self-deceptions and deceptive self-stylizations should be eliminated and one's own historicity must be accepted without illusion.

To the aspects of the principle of openness mentioned so far, with the realization of existence in communication, another aspect is added: the becoming open to the communication partner. The "existential becoming open" (Ph II 64) characterizes the moral basic attitude of the "loving struggle".

---

[19] Cf. Sören Kierkegaard, Abschließende unwissenschaftliche Nachschrift zu den Philosophischen Brocken, 2. part. In: ders, *Gesammelte Werke*, 16. Abt. Düsseldorf, Köln 1958, 55.

The centrality of the principle of openness in Periechontology can be seen in the general characterization Jaspers gives of the "modes of the encompassing." He speaks of "open spaces," or ever-shifting "open horizons," in which the whole expanse of being can manifest its self by any expression. The understanding of reason there is also essentially oriented towards the principle of openness. As the "bond of all modes of the encompassing" (W 113), reason has a twofold task: it must both protect the other modes of the encompassing from narrowing fixations and keep them open to the manifold possibilities of the realization of being.

In Jaspers' *political thought,* too, an understanding of reason closely connected with the principle of openness is central. Thus, for example, in DIE ATOMBOMBE UND DIE ZUKUNFT DES MENSCHEN:

> Reason as the revelation in the origin is the condition of all good. The closedness or the not wanting to be revealed is the actual origin of evil. (AZM 286)

In politics, reason receives the function of bringing about the "new way of thinking" which, despite all egoistic-particular interest politics, is oriented towards the state of world peace or at least towards a temporary world peace order. The "supra-political" reason should permanently influence the old politics in the sense of becoming open for world-wide communication.

Critical considerations on the principle of openness: The multiple references to the principle of openness could easily give the impression that Jaspers overemphasized or even absolutized this principle and thus also the principle of tolerance. Are the following objections raised against him true?

His philosophy is too wide open, because he does not commit himself definitively to anything and thus suggests standpoint-lessness and opportunism in questions of value. If a philosophy is so open and tolerant that it excludes almost no standpoint, then it is also compatible with mutually opposing value standpoints and ultimately leads to value relativism and value decisionism. If a philosophy shies away from rational substantiation of its own value basis out of an exaggerated subjectivism, then it opens the floodgates to arbitrary decisions and prevents the possibility of reasonable criticism of value decisions in the first place.

Philosophies that emphasize the principle of openness and tolerance particularly strongly can be accused of ignoring the paradox of the principle of openness and tolerance out of a naive moralism. This paradox consists in the fact that in absolutizing the principle of openness and tolerance one gives away necessary conditions of the possibility of openness and tolerance. This applies to both the psychological and the socio-political realms. In the psychological sphere, tolerance towards the behavior of a sadistically inclined person must not be limitless, because this would ruin one's own psycho-structure. In the social-political sphere, too, there must be limits to openness and tolerance. This applies to political worldviews and groups that aim to abolish the institutional prerequisites for openness and tolerance, such as freedom of the press, a multi-party system, separation of powers, and so on. Unlimited openness and tolerance would have the effect of opening the door to closed, totalitarian social systems.

Do these objections really meet deficiencies in Jaspers' philosophy or are they based on misunderstandings that he himself has fostered by ambiguous, vague and contradictory statements? This, for example, when he calls for "transcending" the contents of philosophical statements or states that he does not represent a standpoint at all with his philosophy of the encompassing, because the "indirectness of the knowledge of being" only shows itself through the "universal mobility of standpoint" (cf. W 181).

The above-mentioned accusations are not valid in the light of the ethos of humanity emphasized here. From this ethos clear limits of the principle of openness and tolerance can be deduced. These limits lie where this ethos is in principle questioned and endangered. From the point of view of this ethos, there are "enemies"[20] of the principle of openness and tolerance that must be guarded against and fought decisively. With suggestive ideas, these enemies repeatedly address that drive to closedness which the psychologist Jaspers states as a primary need in the human psycho-structure and to which he opposed his idea of humanity.

But the accusation of ignorance in the face of the paradox of openness and tolerance is not true. This is proven by Jaspers' examination of totalitarianism. He saw in totalitarian thinking the main enemy of his own idea of humanity. This is not surprising, since he was directly confronted with the totalitarian exercise of power in the neighboring eastern communist state of the GDR (German Democratic Republic) and, during the period of the "Cold War", with the totalitarian threat posed by the expansionist policies of the Stalinist Soviet Union.

Jaspers' critique of totalitarian ways of thinking did not only concern the ideologies of the totalitarian regimes of the twentieth century. He also had authoritarian and totalitarian ways of thinking in mind, that pose a danger to the maintenance of individual freedom within democratic societies, because they appear with claims to absoluteness and exclusivity. Jaspers fought against such claims with his entire philosophizing: against the absolutization of a being by emphasizing the antinomian basic structure of all being and finally developing his Periechontology; against the absolutization of existence and individual freedom by emphasizing the transcendence-relatedness and the gift character of existence and personal freedom; against the absolutization of the idea of truth by pointing to the equally original plural character of truth-being within the modes of the encompassing (W 605–643); against the absolutization of fact-based scientific knowledge, by invoking the danger of scientific superstition; against the absolutization of religious revelationary content, by drawing attention to the human interpretative component in asserting revelationary truths; against the absolutization of political ideals, by suggesting that such ideals be understood from the outset only as regulative points of approach, and not as conceptions that can actually and finally be transferred into political reality. If one does the latter, ideals degenerate into ideologies with totalitarian, institutional consequences, which Jaspers warningly demonstrated in his critique of totalitarianism (AZM 156–187).

---

[20] "Feinde" here are to be understood in Karl Popper's sense; cf. Karl R. Popper, *Die offene Gesellschaft und ihre Feinde*, Vol. 1 and 2, Tübingen 1992.

Another "enemy" of the ideal of openness and tolerance is a way of thinking that not only belongs to the ideological foundation of every totalitarian rule, but also appears in various political guises. Jaspers subjected it to sharp criticism in the book VOM URSPRUNG UND ZIEL DER GESCHICHTE. It is the conviction that there can be a total view or a complete total knowledge in any field (cf. UZG 164–181).

For Jaspers, the principle limits of openness and tolerance do not have to result in the end of the willingness to communicate and the breaking off of communication with the "enemies" of openness and tolerance. However, one should always be aware of these limits and not fall into an illusory euphoria of openness and communication.

4.6   Personality-Building Values as Educational Ideals

In recent European intellectual history, there has always been an ideal of the university which, in contrast to the self-image of the confessional bound medieval universities, was closely linked to ideas from European humanism and the tradition of the European Enlightenment.[21] The modern idea of the university is expressed in Immanuel Kant's essay DER STREIT DER FAKULTÄTEN (THE DISPUTE OF THE FACULTIES) of 1798 and also in *Wilhelm von Humboldt's* remarks on the tasks of a university, which he wrote down in his "Antrag auf Errichtung der Universität Berlin" (Application for the Establishment of the University of Berlin) in May 1809. It was on *Kant's* and *Humboldt's* ideas that Jaspers based his book DIE IDEE DER UNIVERSITÄT (henceforth also UNIVERSITÄTSSCHRIFT), which he published in 1923 and reissued in revised versions in 1946 and 1961. The latter edition was done in collaboration with his former assistant and later successor on the philosophy professorship in Basel, *Kurt Rossmann*. The fact that Jaspers also published numerous lectures, essays and interviews on the subject proves how continuously he was concerned with the educational institution of the university.

4.7   The University as an Institution of Enlightenment

When Jaspers speaks of the "idea" of the university, he again uses the word "idea" in a regulative sense. As an "idea," the university forms a guideline for thought and action. The approach to this guiding idea is given to the reasonable human being as an infinite, but never finally attainable goal.

Jaspers closely associated the idea of the university with the following concepts: Enlightenment, reason, cognition, science, truth, truth-seeking, education, autonomy, freedom, and morality.[22] In this sense, *Wilhelm von Humboldt* already

---

[21] Cf. Hans-Albrecht Koch, *Die Universität. Geschichte einer europäischen Institution*, Darmstadt 2008.

[22] Cf. Hermann Horn, *Karl Jaspers: Was ist Erziehung? Ein Lesebuch*, München 2nd. ed. 1992, 192–221.

demanded that the university should impart "true enlightenment" and "higher spiritual education" and be "active in establishing enlightenment and morality in the growing generation".[23] *Kant* speaks of the university (especially its philosophical faculty) being concerned with truth and not merely with the usefulness of knowledge. Therefore, the faculty of "free judgement" must be particularly promoted.[24]

Kant and *Humboldt* represent an ethos of enlightenment which, in Jaspers' view, should also characterize the modern idea of the university. This ethos would result in the following requirements for the university: (a) to develop the most differentiated factual knowledge about phenomena in nature and society; (b) to promote the autonomy and self-determination of students by encouraging critical reflection by reason. Critical reflection should not stop at any authority and at any dependence that is not seen through; (c) to convey an attitude of thinking and values that is important for the formation of the students' personality and their worldview (cf. IU 307–334).

4.8   The University as a Mediator of Values for the Formation of Personality

Already in the introduction to the aforementioned UNIVERSITÄTSSCHRIFT, Jaspers emphasizes that university studies should not be primarily orientated on the detailed imparting of knowledge and the most perfect possible professional training (IU 263–264, 405–407). The primary goal must be "the formation of a certain attitude of thinking", which Jaspers calls the "scientific way of thinking" (ibid., 263). Vocational training, he argues, is the duty of the universities of applied sciences, but not of the genuine universities. In this way, Jaspers points to a discrepancy between skill-centered, value-oriented personal education and knowledge-centered, vocationally oriented professional education. In the jointly edited 3rd edition of DIE IDEE DER UNIVERSITÄT, his co-author *Kurt Rossmann* emphasizes how strongly Jaspers' educational-philosophical considerations are orientated towards the ideal type of a value-based personality education:

> It is not the aim of university studies to place students at the disposal of the state and of industry and commerce as perfect scientific specialists with their final examinations. The task and aim of university studies is rather solely to guarantee that self-education in the development of the ability of methodical-scientific thinking and cognition which enables jurists, ... to become a good judge and lawyer, as it does the physician a good doctor, the philologist and historian and the mathematician and natural scientist a good teacher or researcher and scholar. This applies to all professions ... with the exercise of which is connected the demand to be able to cope methodically and scientifically ... with newly arising tasks with hitherto unknown contents. These are the tasks which can arise daily in the practice of all scientific professions and which require, as well as intellectual, ethical

---

[23] Cf. Wilhelm von Humboldt, Schriften zur Politik und zum Bildungswesen. In: *Werke IV*, Stuttgart 1964, 29, 33.
[24] Cf. Immanuel Kant, Der Streit der Fakultäten. In: ders, *Werke in zehn Volumes, Vol. 9*, Part 1, Darmstadt 1963, 290.

decisiveness and responsibility for their solution. To educate to both is the actual task of university studies. (IU 406)

In this programmatic statement, the value dimension of education is explicitly brought to the fore. This also occurs in argumentations where Jaspers himself directly relates the university and the scientific way of thinking to moral value principles. The plea for a "Socratic education" also refers to moral values already mentioned here. This education, Jaspers argues, must be characterized by self-responsibility and recognition of the human equality of students with teachers (cf. ibid., 323–327).

It has been objected to Jaspers that the demand for value-oriented personality formation in university studies is a long-outdated relic of a moralizing intellectual aristocracy. The value-oriented conception of education and science is incompatible with the modern understanding of science. At the latest since the explicit formulation of the value-free principle of the empirical sciences by *Max Weber*[25] at the beginning of the twentieth century, it has become clear that science and values, of whatever kind they may be, must be strictly separated from each other. Doesn't science have to be as value-free as possible? Are the pursuit of science and the communication of moral values not mutually exclusive from the outset?

Such arguments seem plausible at first glance. On closer examination, however, it turns out that the invocation of *Weber* is based on a positivistically narrowed misinterpretation of the principle of the freedom of value judgment of science.

4.9   Principles of Scientific Thinking

There is no doubt that science, and this applies to every scientific discipline, is primarily concerned with obtaining generally valid knowledge that is capable of explanation and prognosis. The humanities, too, must strive for the most objective possible insights and verifiable interpretive hypotheses about the conditions of origin, structures, and functions of cultural works of meaning, if they want to be recognized as sciences and not assigned to the category of producers of creative works of art. This difference is evident, for example, in the distinction between writers on the one hand and literary scholars on the other. With regard to scientific claims of knowledge, the question of truth always arises. Such claims must be true regardless of moral, religious and political standpoints, i.e. they must be able to be accepted as true and generally valid by people of different worldviews and political convictions. In order to arrive at the most objective, true insights possible, a specific method of thinking is required. This is characterized by certain rules or norms to which every scientific effort at knowledge must necessarily orient itself if it should be successful. On closer examination, the rules internal to science turn out to be principles of value

---

[25] Cf. Max Weber, Wissenschaft als Beruf. In: ders, *Gesammelte Aufsätze zur Wissenschaftslehre,* 3. erw. ux Uund verb. ed. Tübingen 1968, 582–613.

internal to science. Jaspers has clearly set them before us in DIE IDEE DER UNIVERSITÄT. They are:

The *principle of truth:* it expresses itself in the search for true statements, regardless of which theory of truth and which criteria are presupposed for the examination of truth claims; Jaspers speaks of an "original will to know", an "unconditional search for truth" and a "knowing as an end in itself", which drives the scientific way of thinking towards ever new efforts at knowledge (cf. ibid., 292–298).

The *principle of unprejudicedness and objectivity:* it requires the avoidance of deliberate falsification of research results, as well as incorruptibility by clients, be they business bosses, politicians, ideological friends or professional colleagues. Jaspers characterized this principle as ability,

> to suspend one's own evaluations for a moment at a time in favor of objective knowledge, to be able to refrain from one's own party, one's own present will, in favor of an unbiased analysis of the facts. Scientificity is objectivity, devotion to the object, prudent weighing; seeking out the opposite possibilities, self-criticism. (ibid., 319)

Insofar as a peculiar education arises at the university, it is *scientific education*. This is determined by the *attitude of scientificity in* general (ibid., 319).

The *principle of intersubjective testability and criticizability of* scientific knowledge claims: these must be able to be recognized and criticized by anyone, if he or she has the necessary expertise. Jaspers states in this regard:

> Scientific attitude is the readiness to accept any criticism of my assertions ... For the thinking person - especially for the researcher and philosopher - criticism is a condition of life. He cannot be questioned enough to test his insight by it. Even the experience of unjustified criticism can have a productive effect. He who evades criticism does not actually want to know. (ibid., 304)

The *principle of conceptual clarity* (cf. ibid., 305): the scientific attitude of thought urges, as Jaspers thinks in another writing, "the clarity of the definite against the vagueness of general speaking, demands concreteness of reasoning" (UZG 88).

The *principle of logical consistency:* it dictates that contradictory statements should not be accepted.

> It is impossible to think and to know when the proposition of contradiction is denied. In the essence of thought lies the recognition of this proposition. He who allows the definiteness of concepts to pass into a fluctuating manifold, and to whom contradiction is not an objection, cannot even speak sensibly. (IU 299)

If these internal value standards of scientific culture are abandoned at the expense of values external to science, such as political-ideological values, then a politicized and ideologized "science" emerges.

4.10   Moral Implications of the Scientific Way of Thinking

If one takes a closer look at the above-mentioned principles intrinsic to science, it turns out that they contain moral implications that go far beyond scientific activity. Jaspers has these in mind when he ascribes to the scientific way of thinking an essential significance for the value-oriented formation of personality.

The principle of truth is necessarily linked to the *moral ideal of truthfulness*. This refers to a moral attitude that forbids scientists to falsify research results and to deceive themselves out of vanity and a desire for recognition. Scientists who are to be taken seriously must be prepared to say goodbye in good time even to pet theories and not to shield them against refutation with all possible immunization strategies.

The principle of objectivity can be fulfilled only gradually, but it presupposes the *moral ideal of tolerance* from the outset. This also applies to the principle of the intersubjective testability and criticizability of knowledge claims. Jaspers emphasizes this ideal whenever he argues for a basic attitude of openness as opposed to closedness. One must be open to and tolerant of alternative theories, i.e. advocate a pluralism of theories. This is a necessary precondition for being able to seriously test one's own hypotheses for their truth value. Alternative viewpoints and theories must be accepted and tolerated as long as the alternatives have not been proven wrong. Intolerance and dogmatism in scientific thinking would prevent the possibility of improving one's own theories or making them even more factual and meaningful by weeding out errors (cf. ibid., 304).

The principle of objectivity and intersubjective testability presupposes the *moral ideal of willingness to communicate*. This ideal suggests communicating openly and publicly with other people, sharing one's own findings honestly with them, always being ready for possible communication and exchange of thoughts. At the university, communication between teachers and students should be on an equal level.

As for the personality formation of the scientific way of thinking, Jaspers states:

> The scientific attitude is more than the promotion of finite cognition. It is education to reason … it promotes humanitas, that is, listening to reasons, understanding, thinking along with the point of view of each other, probity, discipline and continuity of life. (ibid., 320)

The principles inherent in science and the moral ideals associated with them cannot be denied from science, unless science is reduced in the positivist sense in such a way that its humanizing, cultural function and social embedding are lost from view.

4.11   The University and Political Culture

From a narrow, specialized understanding of education and positivistic understanding of science, one must not close one's eyes to the fact that science, its flourishing and its successes, are always related to a cultural environment. This environment can be called the culture of science and education. This form of culture is dependent on the political culture that prevails in a society and determines public life. Where the political culture is dominated by anti-democratic, authoritarian structures and practices, a dirigistic partisan culture of education and science is fostered. Rigid party line thinking and dirigistic planning concepts drastically limit the freedom for alternative thought designs and creative ideas in science. In a non-democratic political system "with total domination" there is no non-partisan university and science.

> For total domination, science, insofar as it is useful, is a means of power. It is not a moment of truth that makes free. Under total domination there can only be training institutes for skilled workers in the broadest sense and for functionaries. (ibid., 286)

Where the political culture is democratic, a pluralistic, liberal educational and scientific culture prevails. In it, there are no politically imposed prohibitions on thought and criticism. The modern idea of the university, in whose tradition Jaspers stands, with its ethos of enlightenment and ideal of humanity, is a constitutive component of the pluralistic-liberal culture of science and education. Without this culture, from a historical point of view, the European exceptional evolution in so many fields would not have come into being. In political and social development, this has led to pluralistic democracy and the Western affluent society, and in the development of knowledge and the advancement of knowledge to the age of computers and digitalization. Concerning the moral development, the demand for respecting and enforcing human rights is closely linked to this cultural tradition; in the legal development, the idea of the rule of law and a global international law is connected with it.

The pluralistic, liberal culture of science with its ethos of enlightenment and humanity, as Jaspers defended it by referring to *Kant* and *Wilhelm v. Humboldt*, is closely related to the political idea of pluralistic democracy and its ideal of freedom. Thus, as Jaspers was deeply convinced, the teaching of scientific thinking at universities also means political education in a humane, liberal-democratic sense.

Transcendence and the Metaphysics of Ciphers Instead of the Belief in Revelation of a Personal God

5

5.1 Transcendence as the Non-representational Ground of Being

For Jaspers, man's existential self-realization is associated with an experience of transcendence. In partial reference to *Kierkegaard's* understanding of existence, he formulates:

> *Existence* is the selfhood that relates to itself and therein to the transcendence through which it knows itself to be given and on which it is founded. (E 113)

Whereas with *Kierkegaard* the Christian God in an act of grace makes possible for the subject the realization of true humanity in the moment of the religious faith relationship, with Jaspers the transcendent point of reference is the transcendence that cannot be further defined in terms of content because it is unthinkable and irrepresentable.

Jaspers uses the word "transcendence" synonymously with "actual being," "absolute being," "actual reality," the "whole of being," the "unity of being," the "ground of all that we are and all that is in itself," the "origin," the "encompassing," "the encompassing of the encompassing," the "Godhead" or "God." As for the encompassing, Jaspers characterizes it as that "wherein all being is for us."

> The encompassing … is not everything as the sum of being, but is the whole that remains unclosed for us as the ground of being. We seek this encompassing when we philosophize. Since it is encompassing, we will not grasp it like a something in the world that occurs to us … but we become aware of it in thinking only as a limit. (W 39)

Jaspers warns against thinking of transcendence in terms of content, because this would "objectify" it and determine its content. In this way, it would cease to be the very last, indeterminable instance from which man experiences himself in his individuality and freedom as "given". *Jeanne Hersch* writes about this:

© Springer-Verlag GmbH Germany, part of Springer Nature 2022
K. Salamun, *Karl Jaspers*, https://doi.org/10.1007/978-3-476-05896-6_5

> Jaspers has occasionally (more often in the late works) called transcendence God. But it is then a hidden God (deus absconditus) who does not reveal himself. Transcendence has absolutely nothing of an empirical being about which one might ask whether it is real – in what space? in what time? ... Transcendence is being, the absolutely encompassing.[1]

Jaspers insists on the methodical demand not to give transcendence or the encompassing a content-related determination under any circumstances, because what is meant by it lies beyond the grasp of our thinking and speaking. With this idea Jaspers takes up an ancient problem of metaphysics again. This arises from the following epistemological consideration: We gain knowledge of the world within the framework of the subject-object split. In this split, the I (subject) faces an object and makes it an object of consciousness. This takes place, as *Kant* emphasized in his epistemology, through formal principles that are given a priori in the human faculty of cognition: the forms of perception (space, time) as well as the categories of understanding (being, nothingness, substance, reality, causality, unity, multiplicity, etc.). However, there are principle limits to the faculty of cognition. It cannot grasp all dimensions of being in categories of thought and language. For *Kant,* this is the "thing-in-itself"; Jaspers cites the "world as a whole" or the "human being as a whole" as examples of these limits. In this sense he often emphasizes: "Man is always more than he can know of himself" (Einf 50), i.e. man possesses a dimension of being that is transcendent. It can never become an object of knowledge through scientific methods, no matter how exact.

Because being cannot be grasped in objective categories, Jaspers assigns the following task to philosophy:

> Philosophy is the thinking assurance of actual being. Because no being that would be given as an investigable object is tenable as the actual being, philosophy must transcend all representationality (Ph I 37).

Does this transcending mean that all informational contents of metaphysical statements have to be relativized? Another important philosopher of the twentieth century and contemporary of Jaspers, namely *Ludwig Wittgenstein*, expressed a similar thought with the "Leitermetapher" (metaphor of a ladder) at the end of his book Tractatus logico-philosophicus:

> My propositions explain by the fact that he who understands me recognizes them as nonsensical in the end, when he has climbed through them – on them – beyond them. (He must, so to speak, throw away the ladder after having climbed up it). He must overcome these propositions, and then he will see the world correctly.[2]

Does that leave only silence about the trans-objective dimension of being, as *Wittgenstein* suggested with the following saying?

---

[1] Jeanne Hersch, *Karl Jaspers. Eine Einführung in sein Werk,* München 1980, 135.
[2] Ludwig Wittgenstein, Tractatus logico-philosophicus. In: ders, *Werkausgabe,* Vol. I, Frankfurt 1984, 85.

What one cannot speak of, one must remain silent about.

Wittgenstein justifies the postulate on silence about the transcendent dimension of being (called by him "the mystical") with the following paradoxical statement:

And how shall we question whether THAT can be expressed which cannot be EXPRESSED?[3]

5.2   Indirect References to Transcendence and the Danger of Mysticism

One possibility to refer at least indirectly to the being that cannot be grasped in linguistic categories has been seen in theology and philosophy of religion in negative paraphrases. So the so-called Negative Theology does not want to say anything positive about God, but only to refer to God with negative statements about what God is not.

In the discussion of Jaspers' understanding of transcendence, attention has been drawn to similarities with *Plotinus'* understanding of being and God. In *Plotinus's* metaphysics, the Godhead is "removed from all contingency and all composition… truly and actually One"[4]and, like transcendence in Jaspers, unknowable, formless, and not comprehensible through thought. As a transcendent "Urgrund" (basic ground) it lies even before the split into subject and object. One has also seen similarities with dialectical theology. For Jaspers, too, attempts to transfer categories that are only applicable to immanent being to the Absolute is possible. The category error made in the process is to be cancelled out by withdrawing the category or by simultaneous use of the opposite category (e.g. the simultaneous designation of transcendence as the absolutely accidental and the absolutely necessary). Thus, by way of logical contradiction and the withdrawal of designations, i.e., by means of foundering thought processes, the Absolute is to be made "present" for moments.

Jaspers tries to solve the dilemma that has been pointed out by not wanting his philosophizing about transcendence to be understood as substantive factual statements. He grants the word "transcendence" and the synonyms used for it only the function of "pointers" (W 153), "conductors" (W 28, 61), "guides" or "ciphers" to the being that cannot be grasped. He only wants to "encircle" this being in "thought processes", to merely "make sure" of transcendence. His metaphysics of transcendence is not to be understood as a doctrine that conveys contents of knowledge about transcendent being, but as a "philosophy" in "abeyance" (W 185). It is supposed to "appeal" to the individual subject to become "certain" of transcendence in his or her own existential fulfilment through an act of existential concern. Jaspers considers the statement "God is" to be the only legitimate verbal formulation with which one can express the experience of transcendence without fixing its content. Whether the word "God" in this statement is merely a "cipher" that is supposed to

---

[3] Ludwig Wittgenstein, Tagebücher 1914–1916. in: ders, *Werkausgabe*, vol. I. Frankfurt 1984, 144.
[4] Plotinus. In: *Plotins Schriften*, Leipzig 1965, 151.

refer indirectly to transcendence without ontological fixation is unclear and controversial in the discussion of Jaspers' metaphysics and philosophy of religion.

The problem of the methodological procedure that Jaspers proposes, however, is that one can easily slide into a speechless mysticism. If every content-related information of used terms has to be taken back ("annulled") by contradictions, circular formulations, etc., the basis for any verbal communication ceases to exist. All that remains is an "eloquent silence", whereby it cannot be determined whether this silence on the part of one or more persons in a communication situation has its origin in the same empathies, associations or intentions. Therefore, contrary to Jaspers' postulate of transcending the contents of his statements, it seems appropriate to take them seriously in their informational content and to establish interpretive hypotheses about them.

The threefold access to transcendence: A crucial problem in Jaspers' metaphysics is the question of access to transcendence. Transcendence does not convey to man any beliefs, moral precepts, or impulses of conscience that he would be responsible to follow. Jaspers mentions three ways in which one can approach transcendence: formal transcendence, existential references to transcendence, and reading the "language" of ciphers (cf. Ph III 36–156).

Formal transcending is described by Jaspers as a process of thinking in which the categories necessarily used in thinking (being and nothingness, possibility and reality, necessity and chance, unity and duality, etc.) have to be thought through to their substantive limits. At these limits, one would be referred "beyond the thinkable to the unthinkable," i.e., transcendence (cf. Ph III 36–53).

As existential references to transcendence, Jaspers names the realization of personal existence in borderline situations and interpersonal communication. These experiences would entail an "inner becoming" of transcendence. In the ascent to existence, the subject experiences an absolute, existential freedom and thus also a "moment" of being given to oneself by transcendence.

From a confessional-theological perspective, the metaphor of being given to oneself has often been interpreted as a secularized notion of being given by the grace of God. From a non-denominational perspective, one can contrast this interpretation with the following interpretation, taking into account the basic liberal structures in Jaspers' thought: Jaspers' point in using the given- or gifted -metaphor and the reference to transcendence is to prevent something that is deeply rooted in the human psycho-structure. It is the tendency to overestimate oneself and to make one's self absolute (cf. PGO 217). In the subjective experience of the moment of absolute personal freedom in the realization of existence, one easily tends to credit this experience as a success of one's own efforts. This presumption would be at odds with Jaspers' ethos of humanity. From the perspective of this ethos the thesis of "being given" by transcendence would take on the function of moderating the egocentric drive to overestimate one's own ego and, in view of the antinomian basic structure of the human being, of appealing to communicative openness and modesty.

5.3   Ciphers as the "Language" of Transcendence

Another turn to transcendence for Jaspers is in the reading of ciphers. The concept of "cipher" is central to both Jaspers' metaphysics and his philosophy of religion. With the "cipher" he takes up an expression by *Immanuel Kant* about the "cipher writing of nature" in his book KRITIK DER URTEILSKRAFT (§ 42). (**CRITIQUE** OF THE POWER TO JUDGMENT).

The cipher is – Jaspers also uses the expression "metaphysical symbol" for it – the expression of the non-representational "language" of transcendence. For Jaspers, an interpretation, in which a cipher is understood as a designation for something that can be more closely defined in terms of its concreteness and scope, is fundamentally not possible.

In metaphorical terms, he speaks of the "possible existence" being capable of "reading the cipher writing" only in the execution of that inner action that brings about the upswing to the realization of selfhood and existence. On the other hand, however, he distinguishes three "languages" through which transcendence can "speak" to existence (cf. Ph III 129–141). The most immediate language of transcendence is experienced in the high moments of existential self-realization; a second language are vivid images and myths in which experiences of transcendence are reflected; a third language is the speculative language of metaphysics. It can also acquire the character of a cipher as soon as what is articulated in its content is not understood as a direct, ontological statement about the absolute being.

About the way in which transcendence "speaks" to possible existence in the ciphers, one only learns that the ciphers become "unambiguous" (Ph III 149) for existence "at the moment of its historical presence". This does not mean univocality in the cognitive-semantic sense, but the uniqueness and unrepeatability of the language of transcendence for the respective individual. In addition, it is also said that the ciphers are always "ambiguous" (Ph III 149), because transcendence neither reveals itself in *one* cipher for *several* human beings in the same way, nor does it reveal itself in *several* ciphers for *one* human being in a comparable way.

> Ciphers are the language of the reality of transcendence, not transcendence itself. They are floating, ambiguous, not universally valid. Their language is not audible to our minds, but only to us as possible existence. (Ch 101)

The indeterminacy of the concept of transcendence in terms of content does not change even if one considers Jaspers' remarks on the "world of ciphers" or the "realm of ciphers" (cf. Ph III 168–181, PGO 251–260, Ch 45–47). There it is only elaborated that in principle everything can become a cipher. Explicitly, Jaspers names nature, art, history, metaphysics, myths, religions, human beings, etc. Given the indeterminacy of ciphers, it is understandable that accusations of vagueness and conceptual obscurity have often been leveled against cipher-metaphysics. Even an otherwise rather benevolent Jaspers- interpreter like the French theologian and philosopher of religion *Xavier Tilliette* came to the conclusion that "the sometimes irritating mysteriousness of Jaspers' Cipher" could not be "remedied" even by the most intensive efforts of interpretation.[5]

5.4   Metaphysics of Ciphers as an Alternative to the Personal Idea of God

In his metaphysics of ciphers Jaspers refers to the idea of God as follows: One has to distinguish between three ciphers of the Godhead. These are "the one God, the personal God, and 'God became man'" (Ch 61).

From Jaspers' point of view, the cipher of the one God is hypostasized in the monotheistic religions to the absolute belief in the only God with all the grievances and evils resulting from it (e.g. violent missionary work, contempt and persecution of non-believers and those of a different faith). For Jaspers, ideas of God in all religions are mere ciphers. This applies to the three monotheistic religions, Judaism, Islam and Christianity, as well as to the natural religions and the pluralistic world of gods of antiquity. The gods and goddesses worshipped there, with their qualities conferred by anthropomorphic projections, merely have the function of referring as ciphers to the entirely non-representational transcendence. What is "experienced" by an individual in the intuitive experience of transcendence via or through a cipher remains inexpressible. It is mystery of the particular existence. In this way, Jaspers has moved the reference to transcendence into the subjective inwardness dimension of the human being, as *Kierkegaard* did with the religious stage of existence. For *Kierkegaard*, the individual upswing into the religious stage of existing means the realization of actual humanity. This, however, only in momentary experiences which, due to the exclusion of past and future by their absolute present, are "transverse to time" and thus allow one to experience "eternity".[6] *Filiz Peach* has written a differentiated study on Jaspers' similar interpretation of momentary experiences as exclusion from objective time.[7]

The cipher-character of myths: Myths have a high value in Jaspers' cipher-metaphysics.[8] He rejects the view of the Protestant theologian *Rudolf Bultmann* that the renewal of the Christian faith must take place by demythologizing the biblical texts. Jaspers' positive assessment of myths is evident from the following quasi-definitional description:

Myth tells a story and expresses "views as distinct from thinking in general terms" (Ent 42); it leads to the resolution of "existential tensions" not through

---

[5] Xavier Tilliette, *Karl Jaspers: Theorie de la verité, Metaphysique des chiffres, Foi philosophique*, Paris 1960, 120.

[6] Cf. Sören Kierkegaard, Abschliessende unwissenschaftliche Nachschrift zu den Philosophischen Brocken, 1. part. In: ders.: *Gesammelte Werke. 16. dept.*, Düsseldorf, Cologne 1958, 187, 197.

[7] Cf. Filiz Peach, *Death, 'Deathlessness' and Existenz in Karl Jaspers' Philosophy*, Edinburgh 2008.

[8] Cf. Werner Schüßler, Die bleibende Bedeutung des Mythos. Zum Mythosverständnis von Jaspers. In: *Jb. der Österreichischen Karl-Jaspers-Gesellschaft*, Jg. 29 (2016), 103–130.

rational cognition but through the telling of a story; it is not an "unambiguous logical entity" and cannot be exhausted through interpretation.

> In mythical figures … symbols speak whose essence it is not to be translatable into another language. They are only accessible at all in this mythical itself, they are irreplaceable, unsurpassable. Their interpretation is not possible rationally, rather their interpretation happens through new myths, through their transformation. Myths interpret each other. (Ph III 132, cf. also: Ent 42)

Thus, for Jaspers, myths are not descriptive worldviews, but value-laden interpretations of the world in which non-rational attitudes, desires, emotions, moods and existential standpoints of meaning manifest themselves. These are more likely to be grasped through an intuitive, "original understanding that carries out evaluations at every moment" than through distancing-analytical intellectual activity (cf. Ent 49–50, 120–123).

Jaspers speaks several times of an irrevocable "spiritual struggle" among the myths. This obviously parallels remarks *Max Weber* made about ultimate value standpoints. *Weber* thinks that

> the different value systems of the world are in an indissoluble struggle with each other … Here … different gods are fighting with each other, and that for all time … And fate rules over these gods and in their struggle, but certainly not 'science'.[9]

Similar to *Weber's* preference for polytheism over monotheism, citing *John Stuart Mill's* liberal stance, Jaspers argues for the plurality of myths. Unlike ideologies and religious faiths, which are dogmatically opposed to each other, myths interpret each other. The plurality of myths, which are in intellectual struggle with each other, entails a mutual questioning and relativization, which prevents the danger of the dogmatization of the myth into an absolutist monomyth. This side of Jaspers' understanding of myth is obviously a result of his fundamental anti-dogmatism.

5.5   Ideas of Gods and Myths as Ciphers of Transcendence and the Rejection of the Demythologization of the Bible

This principle anti-dogmatism also explains Jaspers' attitude in the demythologization-debate with *Rudolf Bultmann*. There he raises the accusation that *Bultmann*, with his existential interpretation of myth oriented on *Heidegger*, ultimately represents not a standpoint of liberality, but of orthodoxy (cf. Ent 61–65). For Jaspers, *Bultmann's* attempt to interpret the event of revelation as a historical call of God to the individual human being is still caught in an orthodox model of revelation of thought and faith. This is because this attempt is based on an illegitimate fixation of transcendence into an objective, historical event of revelation.

---

[9] Max Weber, Wissenschaft als Beruf. In: ders.: *Gesammelte Aufsätze zur Wissenschaftslehre*, 3. erw. Und verb. ed. Tübingen 1968, 603–604.

The main thing that separates liberalism and orthodoxy is their position on the idea of revelation. That God, localized in place and time, once or in a sequence of acts, has revealed himself directly here and only here, is a belief that fixes God to an objective in the world. This is not to be mere reverence from historical bond, but to have the absoluteness of the divine itself. In canonical writings, in confession and dogmas, in the sacrament of priestly ordination, in the Church as the corpus *mysticum* of Christ, and other figures, the revelation and transmission of its grace is bodily present. This revelation is not believed in liberality. (Ent 65–66)

Through the idea of revelation Jaspers sees many possibilities of individual self-understanding and freedom of individual self-realization authoritatively limited. For the sake of the freedom of individual self-determination, there should be no personal-image idea of God, no divine revelation and no associated claim to exclusivity and absoluteness with regard to the contents of faith. When *Bultmann* in his reply to Jaspers' objections against his concept of demythologization said that it seemed not to be clear to Jaspers that

wherever faith in revelation speaks, it asserts, must assert, the absoluteness of the believed revelation, because it understands itself as the answer to: I am the Lord your God. Thou shalt have no other gods beside me! (Ent 93),

By this statement Jaspers only felt confirmed with his criticism of the dogmatism and authoritarianism of any religion of revelation.

The critical arguments against revelatory religions, however, form only *one* side of Jaspers' reflections on religion. Another side manifests itself in the view that in a biblical religion, also in the Christian religion of revelation, many basic existential truths stemming from the Bible are contained. Jaspers is concerned to bring the original, philosophical substance of the biblical faith, i.e. the non-denominational, existential contents of the Bible, to the fore again. One had to release it from the fixed manifestations into dogmatic statements of faith from denominational points of view (cf. Gl. 75–86). With regard to its existential contents myths have a special meaning. With their imagery they symbolically refer to such contents and as ciphers of transcendence indirectly appeal to human beings to appropriate these contents in their own lives.

As always vague and ambiguous ciphers of transcendence, myths are supposed to counteract the tendency to define transcendence rationally and to form "housings" (cages) of objective concepts of God. Because of this positive function of myths it would be wrong to demythologize the Bible in the sense of *Bultmann*. This would mean a reduction of its dazzling wealth of imagery and the impairment of the so vivid, diverse and profound, appellative stories.

5.6   Jesus Is Not Christ, But an Authoritative Figure in the History of Mankind

Myths symbolize fundamental structures of human existence and offer insights into the basic situation (conditio humana) of being human. This is also reflected in the lives and work of the philosophers depicted in the book DIE GROSSEN PHILOSOPHEN.

When Jaspers there refers to *Jesus* as well as *Socrates, Lao-tse* and *Confucius* as an "authoritative human being", he not only rejects the idea of incarnation that is central for the Christian religion. He considers this thought "philosophically impossible" (PGO 270), because it shows Jesus in a wrong light.

> Jesus as reality is a man, historically the last of the Jewish prophets, like them proclaiming, pronouncing God's will, predicting disaster and judgment, demanding repentance. Jesus did not declare himself to be the Messiah, nor did he make himself a sacrament by instituting the Lord's Supper, nor did he found a church. (PGO 54–55)

For Jaspers, the Christian belief in the God-man Jesus Christ obscures the insight into essential existential basic truths that the man Jesus realized in his life and that can become impulses for every human being to shape his own life (cf. GrPh I 214–228). Jesus set a "measure" for people of all times, races, classes, religions, cultures, etc., because as a human being he exemplified the following existential possibilities of being human in a unique way: the ethos of love, meekness and combative unconditionality, the daring to speak the truth and to be true (ibid., 207), the seriousness of the thought of God, the freedom from fear of life, the ability to suffer and the truthfulness of suffering, and finally the ability to die as an answer to the question and fate of death (ibid., 221).

The interpretation of myths as a reflection of the basic situation of being human becomes particularly clear in the book DER PHILOSOPHISCHE GLAUBE ANGESICHTS DER OFFENBARUNG, (PHILOSOPHICAL FAITH AND REVELATION) where Jaspers interprets the myth of *Prometheus*, the myth of the creation of man and woman by God the Father, and the myth of the Fall. In reference to the *Prometheus myth,* he states:

> Prometheus becomes guilty because he does good to man. What makes man to a human being – the knowledge and ability in unlimited possibility of development is connected with guilt. Defiance lies in the origin of man as the act of Prometheus. Man's self-help reflects Prometheus' defiance and his constant 'nevertheless'. From the outset, a moment of defiance runs in the thinking of man and his techne. The mythical cipher illuminates the mystery that becomes present in man's self-consciousness when he asks. Henceforth, every man to whom it has dawned no longer lives only in the simple, beautiful, unquestioning sense of existence, but under ever newly experienced jolts, in the questioning of his being. (PGO 453–457)

In the creation myth of man and woman by God the Father, Jaspers sees the necessary need of human beings for communication represented:

> To be human is not to be alone, but to be with two, in communication. (PGO 460)

The myth of the Fall, interpreted as cipher, says that man did not commit a common crime in his origin, but only that disobedience by which he seizes his own opportunities inherent in him through the likeness of God.

> He can now know, but at the price of becoming mortal. The earth is given over to him for incalculable activity, but at the price of being chased there into infinitely consuming toil.

> This ambiguity of man's existence, his disobedient desire to be known as the condition of his greatness, makes these ciphers point to one side or the other, to the consciousness of doom without consolation in the longing for the lost, or to the enthusiasm of the great task. (PGO 458)

When these passages speak of the ever new questioning of human existence and of the "ambiguity of human existence", Jaspers again refers to the thought motif of the antinomian structure of existence and reminds us that man is confronted with recurring experiences of foundering in his life. Myths have an important enlightening function with regard to man's destiny. They provide insights into the fact that there is no permanent unity or wholeness, no absolute security and total safety; that human existence is ambivalent, contradictory, antinomian divided, or as it is called in the third volume of the existential philosophical magnum opus PHILOSOPHIE:

> … that everything positive is bound to its corresponding negative. There is no good without possible and real evil, no truth without falsity, life not without death; happiness is bound to pain, realization to wagging and losing … in all existence I can see the antinomian structure. (Ph III 221)

Philosophical Faith in Reason as an Alternative to Religious Faith in Revelation

6.1   The Personal Distance to the Christian Faith

To the type of religions of revelation, which Jaspers sharply criticizes, he counts not only Christianity, but also Islam, Hinduism and Confucianism (cf. PGO 130, 223). The criticism starts from the principled distinction between religion and philosophy. For Jaspers, religion is characterized by a "peculiar cult" and an associated community, and is inseparable from myth. Religion, he argues, always includes "man's real relation to transcendence in the form of a sacred being found in the world as one set apart from the profane or unholy." (Gl. 62) In contrast, philosophy knows neither a cult nor a priestly community; it also knows "no holiness in the world exempt from the other world existence." Philosophy means:

> The individual grows up in free, not sociologically real relations, without the guarantee of a community. Philosophy is without rites and without originally real myths. It is appropriated in a transforming way in free tradition. (Gl 62)

This distinction makes it clear that Jaspers gives the concept of religion a clear but relatively narrow meaning. For him, a revealed religion necessarily implies "a direct communication or action of God in space and time, historically localized in certain places" (PGO 173).

Jaspers repeatedly expressed his distance from religious belief in God in autobiographical writings. In a review of his upbringing in his parents' home, there is the remark that he was brought up in the sense of a "liberal worldview", "with only little relationship to church religion".(Aut 112) This relationship was limited to religious instruction at school and confirmation. He comments on the latter as a mere cultural routine:

> When it was time for confirmation, it happened as something belonging to the customs, without religious emphasis, with a feast day that brought purely secular gifts. Confirmation classes were considered fun and ridiculous. (SchW 84–85)

© Springer-Verlag GmbH Germany, part of Springer Nature 2022
K. Salamun, *Karl Jaspers*, https://doi.org/10.1007/978-3-476-05896-6_6

As a primary school student, Jaspers wanted to leave the Protestant church "for the sake of truthfulness". He was prevented from doing so, however, by his father's argument that one should not underestimate the community- and order-creating tradition of the church out of a shared responsibility for the society in which one lives (cf. Aut 112). That the young Jaspers was less contemptuously dismissive of Protestantism than of Catholicism is documented in a passage from a letter to his parents that he wrote from his trip to Italy in the spring of 1903. He was 19 years old at the time, shortly before he learned of his incurable disease. In this letter, he reports on his visit to a festive Easter service in St. Peters Basilica in Rome and comments on his impression of religious rituals in the Catholic Church as follows:

> This morning, on Easter morning, I was in St. Peter's Church to take part in the famous celebrations. But the main thing was that the huge church was filled with an enormous crowd, music and all the rest was nothing outstanding. Cardinal Rampolla was the leader of the hocus-pocus. His clothes were continually changed before the altar, his cardinal's hat was taken off and put back on, and so on.[1]

In later phases of thought, Jaspers often resisted the assumption that his philosophizing was based on a religious point of view. Thus, in PHILOSOPHIE, he programmatically emphasizes that there is a principled, irreconcilable opposition between philosophy and religion:

> The tension vis-à-vis religion is an absolute one: the actually religious can become theologian, but not without rupture philosopher, the philosopher as such not without rupture religious. (Ph I 294)

In a conversation with a Protestant theologian in 1963, Jaspers expressed his distanced relationship to the faith in revelation:

> The faith in revelation has after all the basic character that it cannot be willed and not seen as faith. He who believes, believes by grace. I have not experienced this grace. Therefore, nothing in me urges me to seek this grace. (Prov 1969, 68)

From this it is clear that Jaspers never understood himself as a religious believer. In the last lecture before his retirement in the summer semester of 1961 in Basel, which he gave on the ciphers of transcendence, he made a distinction between a passive and an active agnostic. In doing so, in characterizing both positions, he suggests that he himself could be called an active agnostic (cf. Chap. 10).

6.2   "Catholicity" as a Negative Ideal Type of Faith in Revelation

A very polemical expression of Jaspers' anti-Catholicism can be found in VON DER WAHRHEIT (cf. W 832–868). There he sketches a very negative picture of catholicity, Christian faith and the Catholic Church. In doing so, he counters the negative

---

[1] Suzanne Kirkbright (ed.), *Karl Jaspers Italienbriefe 1902*, Heidelberg 2006, 90.

sides of catholicity with his own understanding of philosophy and reason.[2] Among
the accusations against the Christian faith in revelation are:

The reproach of the *claim to absoluteness:* For Jaspers it is beyond doubt that a
religion that refers to a divine truth of revelation must necessarily assert a claim to
absoluteness for this truth (cf. PGO 53, 222). In doing so, certain truths of faith
would be declared to be wholly indubitable and valid once and for all. Subjective
denial or temporary doubt about the truth claim does not change its absolute validity, because this is guaranteed by God's act of revelation.

In this respect the claim to absoluteness also implies a *claim to generality.* Every
religion of revelation claims that only it is in possession of the knowledge of the
only correct way of salvation. As a consequence of this, Jaspers cites the example of
Christianity as a strategy of appropriation.

> The claim to absoluteness of Christianity, for example, demands that all people should
> become Christians. He is indeed ready to acknowledge all other religions in their truth, but
> only as partial truths, as which they are to integrate themselves into Christianity under
> rejection of the untruths attached to them. He has indeed an attitude of openness for the
> foreign, but in order to discover soon in it only the truth, which is itself Christian. (W 835)

In this context, it is important to note Jaspers' distinction between "unconditionality" and "absoluteness". In contrast to absoluteness, unconditionality concerns existential experiences in the inwardness dimension of the subject. These experiences
cannot be formulated as binding objective knowledge in generally valid statements.
They refer to the uniqueness and unjustifiability of the respective subject. On closer
examination, Jaspers' notion of the unconditional also implies an ethics of mind
component. In certain situations, one must decide and act "subjectively unconditionally" in the sense of "autonomously," i.e., independently of external influences,
life-world impulses, and pragmatic reasons. Jaspers associates a positive sense with
"unconditionality", a negative sense with absoluteness and exclusivity.

The accusation of *exclusiveness:* This refers to the claim to be the sole possessor
of the absolutely true religious doctrine of salvation (cf. Gl. 69–71; PGO 507).

> We call the claim to exclusivity the claim to pronounce or to be the only absolute truth valid
> for all people. ... It lies in the sentence: Apart from the church there is no salvation (extra
> ecclesiam nulla salus) ... The claim to exclusiveness of a faith ... has always been the
> source of discord and of life and death struggle. (PGO 507)

From Jaspers' point of view, the exclusivity of religious belief in revelation is
always associated with a coercive component that implies a missionary zeal. This
becomes clear from the following comparison between the philosophical faith he
propagates and the faith in revelation:

---

[2] Cf. Giandomenico Bonanni, Die Katholizität und ihre Methoden. In: Anton Hügli, Dominic
Kaegi, Bernd Weidmann (eds.), *Existenz und Sinn. Karl Jaspers im Kontext,* Heideberg 2009,
159–186.

We do not speak against God, but against the human claim to represent God. We must speak
out what is true for us: – negative: there is no direct reality of God in the world, speaking in
the world through an instance of office, word, sacrament representing him, to whom obedience is to be rendered by obedience to these offices -, positive: God has created us for
freedom and reason, in which we are given to ourselves, in both responsible before an
instance which we find in ourselves as that which is infinitely more than ourselves and
speaks only indirectly … It is not denial of God that turns against faith in God, but the hidden God against the revealed one. Philosophical consciousness of the reality of transcendence turns against the reality of revelation. (PGO 474)

The accusation of a *wrong understanding of authority:* According to Jaspers,
Catholicism has a wrong and dogmatic understanding of authority:

Catholic authority, from its insight into the nature of authority, demands the obedience of
all. Those who believe it expect, also as a sign of their own truth, that all men will submit
to this self-believed absolute authority. (W 836)

Further criticisms of catholicity are: the pretention of having a total knowledge to
justify the absolute claim to truth and authority; the fixation on a dogmatic idea of
unity, from which only the "One God" is accepted, who has to reveal himself, "as a
single, exclusive authority" (W 841); the doctrine of the Trinity is regarded as
"absurd", as is the idea of the incarnation (Jesus as God's Son) (cf. W 852–853); the
power of Catholic authority does not allow for a "really independent selfhood", it
transforms the individual into a scheme and a type by placing him in a hierarchical
"apparatus". "Being human is coffined." (W 849).
    In his last work on the philosophy of religion, DER PHILOSOPHISCHE GLAUBE
ANGESICHTS DER OFFENBARUNG, the critical argumentation against the Church,
namely that the invocation of a God serves above all power-political goals, is once
again accentuated with particular clarity:

A group of people, the church, makes the appeal to God the means of their worldly power
and self-assertion. The human claim to power disguises itself into the claim of God … It
becomes absolute as the claim of God. The consequence is: through ecclesiastical politics
communication, peace, faithfulness are fatally struck. There is no talking with fighters of
faith. (PGO 160–161)

However, in a footnote Jaspers has relativized the massive criticism of Catholicism
and Christianity insofar as he qualifies: the word "catholic" is … "not to be referred
to the Catholic Church without further ado", what is spoken of would be visible
"everywhere in the world and also in the Catholic Church." This Church as a whole
contained "much more." (W 833) Among this "more" are truths that continually
explode catholicity in the Church. "It lives the truth of the heretics in the Church."
(W 857).
    In Jaspers' view, catholicity and reason are incompatible impulses of life. They
represent "forces" or "powers" of life that are in a constant "struggle" with each
other. This struggle is about mutual clarification of one's own position in each case
and about the central question of which of these standpoints one wants to give preference in one's own life. For a reason-oriented life catholicity is also needed as an

opposing, ideological counter-position. It is supposed to serve as a permanent friction tree against which one can be strengthened by intellectual disputes in the fundamental, existential choice of one's own liberal way of life. With this argument Jaspers partly justifies again the existence of religion (cf. W 861).

The fact that uncritical subordination to ecclesiastical authority can bring about the satisfaction of elementary emotional needs, such as the needs for certainty, security and safety in a superordinate whole, is on the one hand positively acknowledged by Jaspers (cf. W 848). On the other hand, however, this subordination brings about an attitude to life that believes in authority, which is contrary to his ideal of a self-determined, true humanity.

Another argument against religions of revelation is that one can never determine what is the unchangeable, divine revelation and what is merely its theological interpretation (cf. PGO 152–153). As soon as contents of faith are expressed and communicated in the proclamation, they are always already shaped by human views and fixed on quite certain points of interpretation.

6.3 Philosophical Faith in Reason as an Antithesis to Religious Faith

Jaspers sees an important task of his philosophy in clarifying the differences between philosophy, science and religion (or theology). Many passages and chapters in his writings concern this question of demarcation, because he is convinced that philosophy has its own "independent origin" (Aut 114, cf. also PGO 120–121). It is based on an "original will to know". This impulse to know differs from the creative impulses to know in science and from the metaphysical impulses to believe in theology. For the sake of its own origin, philosophy must not be reduced to either science or religion or theology. Jaspers sees the reduction to science as given in logical empiricism or neopositivism. The latter tried to reduce philosophy to the analysis of the language of science and the reconstruction of the logic of science.

There are examples of the reduction of philosophy to religion and theology among Catholic as well as Protestant theologians whenever philosophy is reduced to the rational proof of the contents of faith. Be it that with philosophical arguments one tries to rationally substantiate religious certainty of faith, or be it that philosophy is misused to substantiate the conviction that general-human value ideals would exclusively be constitutive for one's own religious point of view and for no other.

In the Jaspers-discussion, the interest in Jaspers' position on religion is expressed in the following questions: Is Jaspers a philosopher of religion or a religious philosopher? Does he argue from a religious or from a non-religious standpoint? Was he not, after all, a religious believer in some way? Is not the conception of philosophical faith merely a secularized form of religious faith in God?

These questions were often tried to be answered by consulting only Jaspers' writings on the philosophy of existence (sometimes also because the late writings on the philosophy of religion were still unknown). How easy it is to arrive at false or controversial interpretations without considering the complete works is demonstrated by the following examples: The eminent Protestant theologian *Karl Barth*, in his standard work DIE KIRCHLICHE DOGMATIK, interpreted Jaspers' point of view in such a way that he ultimately sees in him a "religious philosopher" in whom, although the "real contents of the Christian tradition" are missing, the philosophizing nevertheless bears "recognizable traces of the closeness of the Christian church and insofar of the Christian space in which it is conceived and designed."[3] The French philosopher *Paul Ricoeur* stated in Jaspers the "paradoxical emergence of a philosophical religion",[4] whereby *Ricoeur* leaves criteria for the demarcation of philosophy, religion and philosophical religion largely open. In contrast, other authors, such as *Hendrik van Oyen,* believe that Jaspers can hardly be called a "religious thinker" because he absolutized human freedom and hypostatized "the subjective-existential actuality of the ego".[5]

By reconstructing Jaspers' position on religion one must take into account autobiographical statements as well as basic structures of his philosophizing as a whole. One should not underestimate, above all, the extensive late work on religion and faith, which falls into the late phase of his thinking and where he explicitly understood philosophical faith as a counter-position and alternative to the traditional, religious faith traditions.

Although Jaspers has repeatedly said that philosophical faith cannot ultimately be "expressed with objective certainty" (cf. VE 94), this faith nevertheless constitutes a fundamental component of meaning in his conception of what it means to be human. This is evident in statements that philosophical faith is a kind of non-objective "certainty of being" and a "confidence in being" of man (cf. W 397). One would misunderstand Jaspers' basic intention if one interpreted philosophical faith as a contemplative attitude in the face of experienced crisis and borderline situations. Nor is it a passive standing firm in the face of negative basic emotional moods such as fear, despair, and experiences of meaninglessness that can arise from manifold experiences of foundering in many ways of life. Rather, this faith represents a highly active attitude to life or living. It is, as *Gerhard Knauss* has rightly emphasized, a specific "philosophical mode of behavior" that is inseparable from a fundamental confidence in life.[6]

For Jaspers' conception of man, philosophical faith is central because it is a necessary condition for individual self-realization. "*Philosophical faith*, however, is man's faith in his possibility. In it breathes his freedom." (Gl. 59) As faith in the principal possibility of being able to experience the upswing to actual selfhood, this faith is at the same time confidence in not falling into resigned despair and nihilistic self-sacrifice when confronted with borderline situations. It represents the basis of

---

[3] Karl Barth, *Die kirchliche Dogmatik*, 3rd vol. 2nd part, Zurich 1948, 134–135.

[4] Paul Ricoeur, Philosophie und Religion bei Karl Jaspers. In: Paul A. Schilpp (ed.), *Karl Jaspers,* Stuttgart 1957, 611.

[5] Oyen, Hendrik van, Der philosophische Glaube. In: *Theologische Zeitschrift*, 14 (1958), 29.

[6] Cf. Gerhard Knauss, Der Begriff des Umgreifenden in Jaspers' Philosophie. In: Paul A. Schilpp (ed.), *Karl Jaspers,* Stuttgart 1957, 139.

meaning from which the human being gains the confidence to go on living and to cope with borderline situations. This optimistic tone is also clear from the following passage:

> The world shows itself to be bottomless. But man finds in himself what he finds nowhere in the world, something unknowable, unprovable, never objective, something that eludes all researching science: freedom and what is connected with it. Here I have experience not through knowledge of something, but through doing. Here the path leads beyond the world and ourselves to transcendence. (Gl 51)

6.4   Philosophical Faith and Universal Communication

For Jaspers, philosophical faith, like reason, must be seen in close connection with the basic communicative concern. This is made clear by statements such as: this faith is "indissoluble from the restless willingness to communicate," or it is "faith in the possibility of understanding each other without restriction." (PGO 211) Just like reason, this faith has the task of constantly spurring on efforts to understand other people and the readiness to communicate, and never letting them flag. This is also true with respect to revealed religions. One should always reflect anew with their advocates on whether there are commonalities between philosophical faith and the respective religion of revelation, for instance in the defense and justification of basic values and human rights. In this sense Jaspers means:

> This philosophical faith, appearing in many guises, does not become authority, not dogma, remains dependent on communication among people who must necessarily talk to each other, but not necessarily pray with each other. (PGO 179)[7]

The communicative dimension of philosophical faith makes it significant for the concern of intercultural understanding. As faith in the human ability to reason it is to support the effort to strive always anew, beyond all ethnic, national, cultural and political differences and contrasts, for a priority world-political goal: the realization of a world peace order or of the world state of peace (see AZM 40–45).

From Jaspers' point of view, one can only approach these goals if one is ready to give up fundamentalist claims to totality, missionary thinking of appropriation and authoritarian ideas of unity in all areas of life. For the philosophical faith the incessant striving for openness, plurality and for an undogmatic way of thinking is characteristic. It is about the readiness to take different personalities, religions, cultures, etc. seriously and to accept them as equal partners in communication.

Jaspers was convinced that the achievement of a state of world peace – and also of a common global ethics, of which there is so much talk – is prevented by the religions of revelation. That is why he also thinks that there is an irreconcilable opposition between philosophy and religion. But this opposition does not exclude

---

[7] Cf: Gregory J. Walters, Jaspers's Philosophical Faith and Revelational Faith Today. Can the Two Faiths Meet in the Stuggle of Human Liberation? In: Richard Wisser, Leonard Ehrlich (eds.), *Karl Jaspers. Philosopher among Philosophers*, Würzburg 1993, 217–227.

that one can meet in religious communities people with whom one works as representatives of a philosophical belief in reason towards common humanitarian and political goals. But then the religious believers must be able to distance themselves from the claims to absoluteness of their religions. Only then they can realize that reason which makes them members of a supra-national and supra-confessional community. Jaspers places great hope in such a spontaneous, unorganized community of reasonable people. This community is to unite people "who can be extremely different in everything else, who can live and feel and want quite differently" (AZM 316) and it is to go "right through all opposites, through denominations, through parties, through states" (AZM 309).

The thoughts on the philosophy of religion presented here show that Jaspers holds neither a theistic nor a consistently a-theistic point of view. The Italian philosopher *Giorgio Penzo,* a pioneer of Jaspers research in Italy, rightly remarks:

> He cannot be considered a theist in the religious sense of the word, since he assumes that divinity is lost when God is fixed in religious belief. For Jaspers, the divine dimension is revealed only in the actual freedom of man. He does not count as an atheist, since his thinking is entirely shaped by the divine, which he defines as transcendence.[8]

Jaspers, as already mentioned, considers himself an active agnostic who, in contrast to the passive agnostic, is interested in the non-objectifiable, existential and transcendent being that lies beyond the boundary of objectively knowable being that can be represented in statements of knowledge (cf. Chap. 10). Therefore, philosophical faith for Jaspers is also faith in an unobjectifiable and unknowable transcendence.

Whether one sees in Jaspers a religious thinker also depends on how narrowly or how broadly one understands the concept of religion. If one understands religion in such a broad sense as in the term "civic religion" in the Anglo-Saxon discussion, if one sees in every idea of transcendence and metaphysics already a religion or the expression of a "religious need", then also Jaspers represents a manifestation of religion. Jaspers, however, as already pointed out, has a narrower concept of religion. Since he never understood himself as a religious philosopher of religion, it is not appropriate to try to adopt him for a Christian standpoint of faith, be it Protestantism or Catholicism.

The autobiographical statements quoted in the introduction and the main thoughts on the philosophy of religion systematically presented here also speak against the following interpretation, which has appeared in a more recent Jaspers interpretation: Jaspers, by reading the Bible again and again, had ultimately "permanently" taken the "standpoint of religion" and he had ultimately accepted for himself "the belief

---

[8] Giorgio Penzo, Der "existentielle Jesus" in Karl Jaspers. In: Richard Wisser, Leonard Ehrlich (eds.), *Karl Jaspers. Philosopher among Philosophers,* Würzburg 1993, 255.

in God as a person".[9] However, this interpretation was later again partly relativized by the mentioned author.[10] Such misunderstandings are also caused by unclear formulations, where the impression arises that Jaspers is presenting his own conviction, although he only tries to reflect the point of view of a religious believer and formulates arguments from this perspective. This also applies to turns of phrase where he speaks of a "cipher of God's helping hand" or the "will of God", thus suggesting a personal interpretation of God. From the overall context of his transcendence and cipher metaphysics, however, such metaphors are probably only to be interpreted as ciphers and not as an expression of religious belief in a personal God.

---

[9] Cf. Bernd Weidmann, Gott als Person – Chiffre der Transzendenz oder mehr? In: *Jb. der Österreichischen Karl-Jaspers-Gesellschaft*, Jg. 26 (2013), 147–166.

[10] Weidmann, Bernd, Einleitung des Herausgebers. In: ders. (ed.), *Karl Jaspers: Der philosophische Glaube angesichts der Offenbarung*. In: *Karl Jaspers Gesamtausgabe*, vol. I/13, Basel 2017, VII–LXXXIII.

On the Meaning of History and the Axial Age in World History

7.1   Different Aspects of the Approach to History

Jaspers distinguished four aspects of dealing with history: the contemporary-historical aspect, the world-historical aspect, the existential aspect and the moral-political aspect.

The *contemporary historical aspect*: (cf. on this also Chap. 9) This is already evident in the early writing DIE GEISTIGE SITUATION DER ZEIT from 1931. Jaspers analyzed there cultural and social tendencies in the interwar period. Like many other contemporary diagnosticians, Jaspers highlights the de-individualization or de-personalization of the human being in an anonymous mass society as a characteristic of the modern age. This age is characterized by science and technology. Other authors who focused their diagnosis of the time on this theme were, for example, the German sociologist *Theodor Geiger* with his book DIE MASSE UND IHRE AKTION (1926), and the Spanish cultural sociologist *Ortega y Gasset* with the well-known book DER AUFSTAND DER MASSEN (1930).

In the 1946 published book DIE SCHULDFRAGE (THE QUESTION OF GERMAN GUILT), Jaspers addresses the Nürnberg trial, which was held against the main exponents of the Nazi regime. He criticizes many of the objections to the trial that were raised in the post-war German public. He also takes a nuanced view of the accusation that all the German people were collectively guilty of the rise of National Socialism.

In his political writings after the Second World War, Jaspers addresses trends and events in German domestic and foreign policy. He deals with the statute of limitations debate of punishing Nazi crimes, argues against reunification and the insertion of an emergency paragraph in the Basic Law. He also criticizes the behavior of the government of the FRG (Federal Republic of Germany) towards the communist Democratic Republic of Germany (DDR) and the formation of a grand coalition in the FRG. He participates in debates on a possible neutralization of the both parts of Germany and discusses current consequences of the "Cold War" between the Soviet Union and the USA for the FRG.

© Springer-Verlag GmbH Germany, part of Springer Nature 2022
K. Salamun, *Karl Jaspers*, https://doi.org/10.1007/978-3-476-05896-6_7

7.2   Four Main Epochs in World History and the Axial Age Thesis

The *world-historical aspect*: This is expressed in Jaspers' thoughts on a "structure of world history" and the division of world history into four main epochs (cf. UZG 39–47):

1. the epoch of prehistory, of which there are found several objects (bones, tools) but no written tradition;
2. the epoch of ancient civilizations in Egypt, Babylonia, China, India and in cultures around the Mediterranian;
3. the epoch of the Axial Age, during which important cultural achievements of mankind were produced in various parts of the world;
4. the epoch of the scientific-technical age, which was created by the development of modern European science and technology.

The thesis of an Axil Age in world history is generally regarded as Jaspers' most important historical-philosophical assumption, which is closely related to his "humanistic credo".[1] He assumes that there has been a serious break in the history of mankind so far, which he calls the "Axil Age". By this he means an empirically definable period of time in which the basic categories of thought and the beginnings of the world religions emerged almost simultaneously. This period lasted from about 800 to 200 B.C. At that time in China, India and the Occident – by the Occident Jaspers does not only mean Greece, but also Palestine and Iran – important cultural foundations and categories of thought were created. They have an effect up to the present time and still substantially determine the life of people in the modern age. As outstanding historical personalities, who have worked innovatively in this epoch, are cited:

> In China lived Confucius and Lao-tzu, developed all directions of the Chinese philosophy, thought Mo-Ti, Tschuang-Tse, Lie-Tse and uncounted others, – in India the Upanishads were created, lived Buddha, there were developed all philosophical possibilities up to the scepticism and up to the materialism, up to the Sophism and up to the Nihilism, as in China, – in Iran Zarathustra taught the demanding world view of the struggle between good and evil, – in Palestine the prophets appeared from Elijah to Isaiah and Jeremiah to Deuterojesaias, – Greece saw Homer, the philosophers Parmenides, Heraclitus, Plato – and the tragedians Thucydides and Archimedes. All that is only indicated by such names grew up in these few centuries approximately simultaneously in China, India and the Occident, without knowing each other. (UZG 17–18)

Jaspers is considered as the inventor of the term "Axial Age". He first used it in a lecture about the spiritual state of Europe, which he gave at the *Recontres Internationales* in Geneva in September 1946.[2] With the "Axial Age", he wanted to

---

[1] Aleida Assmann, Jaspers' Achsenzeit, oder vom Glück und Elend der Zentralperspektive in der Geschichte. In: Dietrich Harth (ed.), *Karl Jaspers. Denken zwischen Wissenschaft, Politik und Philosophie*, Stuttgart 1989, 194.

[2] Cf. Stefania Achella, Europa – wohin soll es gehen? Jaspers at the Recontres internationales de Genève (1946). In: *Jb. der Österreichischen Karl-Jaspers-Gesellschaft*, Jg. 26 (2013), 87–116.

design a historical-philosophical "world-historical scheme" that could give "meaning" to empirically explorable, particular historical events and concern "humanity as a whole" (cf. UZG 247–248). On the one hand, Jaspers is aware that his design is an ideal-typical construction, but on the other hand, he also notes that this scheme "seems to correspond most closely to the demands of openness and unity and to empirical reality today." (UZG 241) However, he does not clearly specify to what extent the Axial Age is to be understood as a historically verifiable, empirical fact or as a historical-philosophical, speculative construction of meaning.

As a criticism of the Axial Age thesis, it has been argued, among other things, that the time-frame given by Jaspers for the Axial Age is untenable. For example, *Alfred Weber*, from whom Jaspers borrowed many thoughts and terms for his Axial Age thesis, assumed the period of revolutionary, cultural upheaval in world history to be from the 9th to the sixth century B.C.[3] *Jan Assmann,* a cultural scientist and Egyptologist from Heidelberg, is of the opinion that there were already revolutionary upheavals in Ancient Egypt with similar structural characteristics to those highlighted by Jaspers with the Axial Age. Furthermore, Jaspers has neglected the transition from oral to written tradition, which essentially determined the formation of a cultural memory in the Axial Age cultures.[4]

The world-historical perspective manifests itself in Jaspers' oeuvre not least in the great and unfinished late project of a world history of philosophy. With the political goal of a world peace order or a state of world peace, he also thought on a world scale. The plea for a world order in the form of a "federal community of states" instead of a "totalitarian world empire" is also to be mentioned here (cf. UZG 191–199).

The *existential aspect*: This aspect of Jaspers' philosophical approach to history becomes evident in his reflections about the historicity of man and the meaning of history. This involves both the fact that the human being is always a component of history, and the significance of history for individual self-realization. In this context, Jaspers considers the existential appropriation of the form of life and thought of historical personalities to be significant. The subjectivity aspect in the experience of history is considered as an essential reference to the uniqueness and irreplaceability of each individual. In existential philosophical thought, the concept of historicity refers both to the inescapable being-in-situation (cf. Ph II, 201–203) of the human being and to the non-empirical dimension of existential self-realization (cf. Ph II, 118–149).[5]

---

[3] Cf. Alfred Weber, Kulturgeschichte als Kultursoziologie [1935]. In: *Alfred Weber-Gesamtausgabe,* vol. 2, Marburg 1997, 67.

[4] Cf. Jan Assmann, Ma'at: Gerechtigkeit und Unsterblichkeit im Alten Ägypten, München 1990, 41–50; Jan Assmann, Das kulturelle Gedächtnis: Schrift, Erinnerung und politische Identität in frühen Hochkulturen, München 1992, 195, 290–202.

[5] Cf: Otto Friedrich Bollnow, Existenzphilosophie und Geschichte. Versuch einer Auseinandersetzung mit Karl Jaspers, in: Hans Saner (ed.), *Karl Jaspers in der Diskussion,* München 1973, 235–273.

7.3   History Has No Immanent Meaning

Part of Jaspers' understanding of history is the view that there is no immanent meaning in history. A result of this view is his fundamental rejection of deterministic views of history.[6] He vehemently denies that there are certain regularities for the course of history, through the study of which one can predict the future course of the historical process.

> The question of the meaning of history cannot be solved by an answer that expresses it as a goal. Every goal is a particular, provisional, outdated one. To construct history as a unique history of decision in the whole always succeeds only at the price of neglecting essentials. (EiPh 81–82)

Jaspers also refers to that phenomenon which has been called "self-fulfilling" and "self-destroying prophecy" in the human and social sciences.

> But there is no statement about the future, insofar as human will is involved in its coming about, that would not be or could not become a contributing factor. The statement drives towards something or deters. In particular, the supposed knowledge of a future is a factor in bringing it about. (UZG 144)

Jaspers defends the non-deterministic view of history, according to which the future is in principle "open" against deterministic theories by *Arnold Toynbee, Oswald Spengler* and *Karl Marx* (cf. UZG 14, 175, 238). His consistent indeterminism follows already from the basic philosophical-anthropological assumption that individual freedom and personally attributable responsibility are central to the existential realization of human beings. This assumption necessarily presupposes an "open" course of history. A predictable final state, such as the decline of the West in *Spengler's* view, or the attainment of a final state of social salvation in *Marx's* (classless society), cannot exist from this perspective. The further course of history depends on the reasonable and responsible actions of individual human beings. Each person must himself set the meaning and seize the open possibilities in order to advance the future development of history towards more freedom, humanity, mutual understanding and universal communication (cf. UZG 215–218, 235–238, 240–244).

From his existential-individualistic basic view, Jaspers also deals with science and technology as essential driving factors of history. In the historical epoch of the modern age, science and technology are of the utmost importance. On the one hand, he emphasizes the far-reaching positive consequences of the development of science and technology for all areas of life. On the other hand, however, he warns against an exaggerated faith in technology and an uncritical superstitious belief in science, which sees in science a universal instrument of solution for all problems. At the same time, however, Jaspers distances himself from any demonization of

---

[6] Cf. Kurt Salamun, Einleitung des Herausgebers. In: ders. (ed.), *Karl Jaspers. Vom Ursprung und Ziel der Geschichte.* In: *Karl Jaspers Gesamtausgabe,* vol. I/10, Basel 2017, XII–XIV.

technics, as he sees it in the writings of *Friedrich Georg Jünger.*[7] The further development of technic and its consequences depend decisively on the value attitudes and value decisions of individuals. Jaspers clearly expresses his own assessment of technology when he states:

> Technology is only a means, in itself neither good nor evil. It depends on what man makes of it, what it serves him for, under what conditions he places it. (UZG 121)

The *moral-political aspect*: That this aspect is associated with Jaspers' conception of history becomes clear in connection with the Axial Age thesis. By making people aware of this world-historical period, he wants to point to the common framework of a historical self-understanding for peoples with different cultural and political traditions. The awareness of the Axial Age is intended to overcome the narrow-minded particularism and the separating exclusivity claims of political, ideological, cultural, religious and national standpoints in the present.

7.4   The Axial Age Thesis in Context of the Danger of an Atomic War

A historically founded, mutual understanding between the peoples is an indispensable precondition, so that mankind can save itself from the universal borderline- and crisis- situation, which has arisen through technical progress. With the atomic bomb age, a completely new age has dawned for all mankind. By awakening the consciousness of a common origin of history in the Axial Age, Jaspers hopes to achieve a turnaround among political leaders towards a reason-oriented, morally impregnated politics. Only such a turn could save humanity from nuclear war.

Jaspers developed the thesis of the Axial Age during the phase of the "Cold War" in world politics. This phase was marked by the confrontation between the two superpowers of the time, the United States and the Soviet Union. The book containing the Axial Age thesis was completed in August 1948, after Jaspers had moved to Basel in March. In the spring of 1946, American President *Harry S. Truman* had threatened *Josef Stalin* with serious consequences, up to and including the use of nuclear weapons, if the Soviet Union did not withdraw the Red Army from the occupied oil-rich territories in northern Iran.

The danger that the confrontation between the two superpowers could lead to war again worried Jaspers deeply at the time. Should the Soviet Union win the world political competition and the totalitarian Soviet-Russian model of society would win the day, this would be the end of everything Jaspers had always had in mind as the ideal of what it means to be human. This ideal, he was convinced, could only be realized, at least partially, in a liberal-democratic model of society. In order to come closer to the realization of this ideal, politics in the world, which up to now has everywhere been only power- and interest politics, would have to be reshaped by a supra-political, by a "moral idea" and by an ethos dominated by reason (cf. AZM 49–57).

---

[7] Cf. Friedrich Georg Jünger, *Die Perfektion der Technik,* Frankfurt 1946, 96–97.

World History of Philosophy and Vision of a "World Philosophy"

8

8.1 History of Philosophy in World Historical Perspective

Only one volume of the great project of a history of philosophy from a world-historical perspective was published during Jaspers' lifetime: the extensive book DIE GROSSEN PHILOSOPHEN (THE GREAT PHILOSOPHERS) from 1957, in which *Socrates, Buddha, Confucius* and *Jesus* are named as the "authoritative people" in the history of philosophy. For Jaspers they are

> people who, through their existence and being, have historically determined the human condition like no other people. They are witnessed by an effect that has lasted through millennia until today … One may hesitate to call them philosophers at all. But they have become the basis of tremendous philosophical movements of thought. (GrPh 46)

The fact that Jaspers was intensively involved with Asian thinkers and founders of religions has several reasons. One of them is related to his life story. During the Nazi regime and the ban on teaching and publishing, a close, friendly relationship developed between him and *Heinrich Zimmer*. The latter was a colleague at the University of Heidelberg and a specialist in Asian cultures, in particular the culture of India. He found himself in the same life situation as Jaspers. Both lived in a "racially mixed marriage" condemned by the National Socialists. Zimmer, like Jaspers, was married to a woman of Jewish origin and stood by her even under the pressure of National Socialist propaganda. His wife had a famous name in the German-speaking cultural scene. She was the daughter of the writer *Hugo von Hofmannsthal.*

Hans Saner, the co-editor of the correspondence between Jaspers and Zimmer, reports the following about *Zimmer*'s influence on Jaspers:

> Jaspers began to study Far Eastern cultures from about 1938 and *Zimmer* brought him writings on Chinese and also Indian and Japanese philosophy, literature and history for this

© Springer-Verlag GmbH Germany, part of Springer Nature 2022
K. Salamun, *Karl Jaspers*, https://doi.org/10.1007/978-3-476-05896-6_8

purpose. *Zimmer* became important to Jaspers during this period as an interlocutor and as an extremely stimulating 'teacher'.[1]

In his AUTOBIOGRAPHIE Jaspers writes about this time, in which he had to experience being "excluded in his own state", that his "historical interest experienced a transformation" (cf. Aut 120).

In retrospect, he cites another reason for turning to Asian thought. In view of the totalitarian rule of National Socialism, it occurred to him whether "spirits" in "occidental history" had not in some way "paved the way for making such horror possible". In contrast to it, it was important for him to work philosophically "on the preconditions for the possibility of universal communication" (cf. Aut 121). Individual, interpersonal communication, which was the focus of his existential philosophy, had to be extended to a reasonable, universal communication. Human ideals from non-occidental cultures should also be included into this ideal. This explains the extensive discussion of Indian and Chinese thinkers and founders of religions, such as *Buddha, Nagarjuna, Lao-tse* and *Confucius* in DIE GROSSEN PHILOSOPHEN.

For Jaspers, engaging with great thinkers from the past means not just reading lore, but a subjective process of appropriating their thoughts. In dealing with the texts, one should "allow oneself to be addressed in a personal orientation." (GrPh 60) The understanding thought processes would have to reach beyond the rational efforts of interpretation into the deep dimension of personal concern and engaged co-experience. "The philosophical truth" of the thoughts of the great thinkers

> does not already become clear in their abstractions and schematizations into doctrinal pieces ... Appropriation does not succeed in the merely rational, but with its help only in dealing with the great ones themselves ... They are members of a realm of spirits in which each is wholly and uniquely and yet all are in communication of sense with one another, ... They speak to us in that one points us to the other. A merely aesthetic contemplation isolates and enjoys; philosophical contemplation connects and transforms into its own reality. (GrPh 71–72)

In this passage, Jaspers once again addresses the philosophia perennis as a body of basic philosophical questions, problems, and truths that are necessarily connected to the conditio humana. These basic questions are important at all times. They must become the subject of philosophical reflection and existential appropriation in different times from different perspectives, in different cultures, and from different life situations. They include questions about the meaning of life, about birth and death, about moral standards of humanity, about commitment to ancestors and tradition, about transcendence or God, about the role of knowledge in human life (cf. WGP 55–57).

---

[1] Hans Saner, Zwischenbemerkung. In: *Karl Jaspers, Heinrich Zimmer: Briefe 1929–1939,* ed. by Maya Rauch and Hans Saner. In: *Jb. der Österreichischen Karl-Jaspers-Gesellschaft,* Jg. 6 (1993), 15.

8.2   The Multi-Aspectual Concept of the World History of Philosophy

Jaspers does not want his world history of philosophy to be understood as a canon of knowledge that can be learned, in which the world wisdom from the history of philosophy to date is encyclopedically summarized. Rather, it is intended to be a fund of thoughts and thought processes that can be individually acquired, which thinkers and cultural creators with philosophical depth have contributed to world culture. As documented by two volumes of fragments, notes and short descriptions (cf. Nachlass 1 and 2), this project was virtually enormous.

In the GROSSEN PHILOSOPHEN, still published by Jaspers, there are extensive chapters on the "generative founders of philosophizing", examples of which are: *Plato, Augustine and Kant.* From the "origin thinking metaphysicians" are, among others, *Heraclitus, Parmenides, Plotinus, Spinoza, Lao-tse* and *Nagarjuna.*

In the fragments of the Nachlass, *Pascal, Kierkegaard, Lessing* and *Nietzsche* are treated fragmentarily as "great awakeners". Jaspers singles out *Dante, Shakespeare, Goethe, Hölderlin, Dostoyevsky* and *Racine* as "philosophers in poetry". As "Philosophers in research" are mentioned *Einstein, Max Weber,* and *Jacob Burckhardt,* as "Philosophers in political thought" *Machiavelli, Thomas More, Locke* and *Tocqueville.*

According to Jaspers' plan, the future world history of philosophy should be structured according to poly-aspectual viewpoints:

1. a *personal aspect,* that is, a world history of philosophical personalities; this is the published volume DIE GROSSEN PHILOSOPHEN,
2. a *structural aspect,* that would be a world history of thought forms, in which the categories and methods of philosophizing would be treated,
3. a *historical-chronological aspect,* that would be a world history of philosophy in different cultural areas and epochs,
4. a *factual aspect,* this would concern the worldwide contents of philosophy,
5. the *genetic aspect,* which deals with the origin of philosophy in myth, language, religion and art, and
6. the *pragmatic aspect,* this would be the question of the effect and practical realization of philosophy (cf. WGP 113–120).

8.3   The Vision of a Future "World Philosophy"

Late in his life, Jaspers sometimes spoke of a "world philosophy" that would have to build on the world history of philosophy.[2]

---

[2] Cf. Hans Saner, Jaspers' Idee einer kommenden Weltphilosophie. In: Leonard H. Ehrlich, Richard Wisser (eds.): *Karl Jaspers Today. Philosophy at the Threshold of the Future,* Lanham, MD 1988, 75–92; Hans Saner, Karl Jaspers on World History of Philosophy and World Philosophy. In: Kurt Salamun, Gregory J. Walters (eds.), *Karl Jaspers's Philosophy: Expositions and Interpretations,* Amherst, New York 2008, 89–113.

In the obituary he wrote about himself during his lifetime, you will find the passage:

> He gave all the strength of these years to the continuation of his philosophical work, which in itself was unfinishable, with which he wanted ... to participate in the task of the age, to find the way out of the end of European philosophy into a coming world philosophy.[3]

That Jaspers wrote his own obituary, which *Hans Saner* read out at the funeral, may seem unusual. *Saner* justifies this by referring to an old custom in Basel for citizens to write their own obituaries.

A look at Jaspers' complete works shows that the word "world philosophy" only rarely appears in them. It is first found in 1951 in a Basel radio lecture where he sets out his own path to philosophy. The well-known metaphor from this lecture reads:

> We are on the way from the sunset of European philosophy through the twilight of our time to the dawn of world philosophy. (RAu 391)

How Jaspers arrived at the term "world philosophy" cannot be clearly reconstructed. Nor is it clear what exactly he meant by it. Perhaps the choice of this word is an analogy to the word "world literature", as he used it in one of his interpretations of *Goethe*. In a lecture given in Basel in 1949 entitled *"Goethes Menschlichkeit"* (Goethe's humanity), the passage can be found:

> Goethe coined the word "world literature". He saw the advent of the spiritual intercourse of peoples, showed poets, critics, writers, researchers and philosophers the task of knowing each other and listening to each other. One should tolerate each other when one feels foreign, love each other as belonging to the one spiritual space in which universally human popular poetry grows everywhere, and in which the rare great works of individuals stand valid for all. He grasped the unity of humanity with the thought of world literature. (RAu 79)

It has been suggested that one motivation for the choice of the word "world philosophy" may also have been Jaspers' longing for a cosmopolitanism and the striving to overcome nationalistic ideas. Jaspers also associates the word "world philosophy" with the idea of "a unity of mankind." This is not concerned with a political unity, but with a "spiritual" or intellectual unity. By this Jaspers means a "spiritual space" in which universally human, philosophical reflections arise everywhere in the world, and in which the rare great works of individuals "stand there validly for all" who are willing to appropriate these reflections in a process of existential understanding. In the Nachlass-Schrift WELTGESCHICHTE DER PHILOSOPHIE. EINLEITUNG (WORLD HISTORY OF PHILOSOPHY, INTRODUCTION) one can found the sentence, "The *idea of a coming world philosophy* is inevitable." (WGP 76) In this context, there is also talk of a "universal philosophy" as an "organon of reason" and a "comprehensive systematics of the possibilities of thought", as well as of a "coming philosophy of the earth's circle".

---

[3] Hans Saner (ed.), Karl *Jaspers. Was ist der Mensch? Philosophisches Denken für alle*, München, Zurich 2000, 66–67.

A passage from the context in which Jaspers emphasizes the inevitability of a future world philosophy is the following:

> The idea driving a history of philosophy, however, remains to make perceptible a maximum of unity in the thought and in the image, which shows itself in the openness of understanding and the continued communication and willingness to communicate, not in the conclusion of a known. The whole is to be found neither in the universal nor in a truth that could be discovered by us somewhere in the world as the only truth, to which one might convert oneself or which one might claim as one's own revelation for all. (WGP 76)

That world philosophy, together with p*hilosophia perennis* and the Axial Age in World History, are dominant parts of the central guiding idea that Jaspers has always pursued with his philosophizing is obvious. It is the basic appeal to realize interpersonal communication and the aforementioned goal that there must be universal communication among all people across all political, cultural, and religious boundaries. Only in this way could the universal atomic bomb danger be eliminated and a continuous state of world peace be achieved.[4]

---

[4] For further attempts to interpret Jaspers' idea of a world philosophy, cf. besides Saner's interpretations also: Andreas Cesana, Karl Jaspers' Idee einer Weltphilosophie und das Problem der Einheit des Denkens. In: Reinhard Schulz, et al. (eds.), *"Wahrheit ist was uns verbindet"*, *Karl Jaspers' Kunst zu Philosophieren*, Göttingen 2009, 315–328; Anton Hügli, World Philosophy: On Philosophers making Peace. In: Helmut Wautischer, Alan M. Olson, Gregory J. Walters (eds.), *Philosophical Faith and the Future of Humanity*, Heidelberg, London, New York 2012, 335–345.

Provocative Statements on German Policy of His Time

9.1   The Path to Politics

In the Autobiographie, Jaspers reports that he was already confronted with politics in his family as a child. As mentioned in the biographical section of this book, Jaspers' grandfather and two of his mother's brothers were members of the state parliament in Oldenburg, and his father was chairman of the Oldenburg city council for decades. An uncle, Theodor Tantzen, was twice Minister President of the Free State of Oldenburg before Oldenburg was incorporated into the region of Lower Saxony after World War II. Jaspers writes about the participation in politics in his youth:

> I myself took part in all these things only as a spectator, although I sometimes took a lively part in the discussions in the family. My basic attitude until 1914 was quite apolitical. (Aut 65)

In an interview, which Jaspers gave in 1962, he stated looking back on this period before the First World War:

> How irresponsible almost all of us were at that time: government and politics were simply objects of contempt to us, suitable objects for the pictures and words of the splendid "Simplizissimus" in Munich ... politics was none of our business. I took an unwitting part in the political irresponsibility of the German mind. (Prov 149–150)

A change in the view of politics occurred in 1914 at the beginning of the First World War. In the Autobiographie there is a reference to the fact that from this year onwards Jaspers was strongly influenced by *Max Weber* in his assessment of politics. Weber, he says, introduced him to "national thinking," which had hitherto been alien to him, and Weber pointed out to him the responsibility that Germany had as a land of great power to prevent "the world from being divided between Russian knout and Anglo-Saxon convention." Here a messianic, national keynote is sounded when it goes on to say:

© Springer-Verlag GmbH Germany, part of Springer Nature 2022

K. Salamun, *Karl Jaspers*, https://doi.org/10.1007/978-3-476-05896-6_9

> Our task and chance is to save the third between the two, the spirit of liberality, of freedom
> and diversity of personal life, of the greatness of Western tradition. Such was Max Weber's
> spirit, in which I now took part. (Aut 66)

In a biographical note that Jaspers had to write in 1946 for the American military
authorities in Württemberg-Baden before his reinstatement at the university, he
reports that he had been a member of the German Democratic Party from 1919 to
1923, but had never belonged to a political party after that.[1]

The aforementioned messianic, national undertone is still echoed in post-war
political writings, where the possibility is considered that a free democratic Germany
to be rebuilt after the National Socialist catastrophe, could become a worldwide
model, when the "transformation" of power-political thinking into a "moral-political
way of thinking" had taken place. The interest in politics awakened by *Weber* also
found expression in membership in a political club between 1915 and 1923. The
cream of the Heidelberg professoriate frequented this club. Lectures were given and
the consequences of the First World War were discussed. Despite the example of
Weber – who was publicly involved in national-liberal and left-liberal political
groups – Jaspers had a certain shyness at that time to speak and write about politics
in public.

> Neither in the First World War nor afterwards did I speak of political things in my lectures
> or in writings. I had a shyness because I was not a soldier. For politics is about the serious-
> ness of power founded on the stakes of life. I lacked legitimacy. The shyness diminished as
> I grew older. Mainly because in the twenties I saw the obvious political failure of the sol-
> dierly. I recognized the false political claim in it. (Aut 71)

After his personal experience with the National Socialist system of rule, his attitude
towards politics changed fundamentally. This was correctly recognized in the
Jaspers discussion by the political philosopher *Dolf Sternberger*. He stated that only
the experience of Hitler's dictatorship had made Jaspers a "political philosopher".[2]

In a *self-portrait* Jaspers confirmed this:

> Politics is a reality which burns on our nails! It determines our existence. We are dependent
> on it. That only became clear to me with National Socialism. I probably began to concern
> myself with politics as early as the twenties: In my "Spiritual Situation of the Times"
> (1931). But the Nazi era was decisive. (SchW 35)

After the Second World War, Jaspers commented on current political events and
problems in television interviews, newspaper articles and book publications. He
discussed questions of German domestic and foreign policy as well as the world
political constellation of the time in the Cold War period between the USA and the
Soviet Union. His views were controversially discussed in the German press and
were often perceived as a provocation of the political "Zeitgeist" of the time.

---

[1] Karl Jaspers, Karl Heinrich Bauer, *Briefwechsel 1945–1968,* Heidelberg, New York 1983, 7.
[2] Cf. Dolf Sternberger, Jaspers und der Staat. In: Hans Saner (ed.), *Karl Jaspers in der Diskussion,*
München 1973, 418.

The writings in which Jaspers discussed current political issues at the time, that will be discussed now, are in chronological order: DIE SCHULDFRAGE (On Germany's Guilt and Political Liability) (1946); VOM URSPRUNG UND ZIEL DER GESCHICHTE (1948); DIE ATOMBOMBE UND DIE ZUKUNFT DES MENSCHEN (1958); FREIHEIT UND WIEDERVEREINIGUNG. ÜBER AUFGABEN DEUTSCHER POLITIK (1960); HOFFNUNG UND SORGE. SCHRIFTEN ZUR DEUTSCHEN POLITIK 1945–1965 (1965); WOHIN TREIBT DIE BUNDESREPUBLIK? TATSACHEN – GEFAHREN – CHANCEN (1966); ANTWORT. ZUR KRITIK MEINER SCHRIFT ,WOHIN TREIBT DIE BUNDESREPUBLIK?' (1967).

About the early writing DIE GEISTIGE SITUATION DER ZEIT (1931) there is no agreement in the Jaspers-discussion whether it should be qualified as a political writing or not.

9.2 "The Intellectual Situation of the Time" as a Precursor of Political Criticism in the Post-War Period

The small book DIE GEISTIGE SITUATION DER ZEIT (THE INTELLECTUAL SITUATION OF THE TIME), which appeared as volume 1000 in 1931 in the then widely distributed "Sammlung Göschen", is often underestimated in its political message. Because of its title, it has been regarded merely as an a-political analysis of the intellectual and cultural situation of the late twenties of the twentieth century in Germany and other European countries. Jaspers subsumes these countries together with the USA under the term "Occident". Contributing to the verdict that the book was a-political was the accusation that Jaspers nowhere referred in it to the political movement of the National Socialists. At that time, this movement had already made itself strongly felt in the German public through tightly organized marches and loud propaganda against the Weimar Republic. In the preface to the 1946 edition, Jaspers justifies himself as follows:

> This book was written in 1930. I had little knowledge of National Socialism at that time, somewhat more knowledge of Fascism. In the satisfaction of having just finished the manuscript, I was astonished and shocked at the September elections of 1930, the first success of the National Socialists at that time. The manuscript remained lying for a year, as I did not want to let it go to the public without my PHILOSOPHIE, which appeared in three volumes in 1931 a few weeks after this writing. (GSZ 194)

Certainly, the book contains primarily a general critique of culture and civilization. To that extent, one could consider it a-political. But then one would overlook the fact that the main intention of the book was a political-humanitarian concern. Jaspers wanted to warn of the dangers associated with the advancing development of technology and the social tendency towards mass societies. The freedom of the individual was endangered when it was fitted into a "universal order of existence" and subjected to the "principle of mechanization" of all areas of life. If Jaspers had already warned in the PSYCHOLOGIE DER WELTANSCHAUUNGEN that man might submit to the "spirit of rationalism" and thereby become entangled in the "housings" (cages) of "rational worldviews" and institutions. Here he continues the critique of rationalism in the sense of Weber's demythologization thesis.

As the main reason for the de-personalization and leveling of individuals into "mass people", Jaspers cites a "nowhere stopping rationality". This forces existence into "calculability" and "technical control" and promotes "calculation" in economic decisions "up to the rationalization of all action". (GSZ 17–18) In the sense of Weber, Jaspers speaks of the "de-godification of the world" to which the natural sciences have also contributed decisively "with their rationalization, mathematization and mechanization of the world" (cf. GSZ 21). Through this, a "technical mass order" has emerged, to which people are subjected as citizens.

Mass existence is expressed in the fact that the individual is no longer "himself". He is only there to perform a function in the masses and to adapt to mass needs and mass activities. One does what most do, one buys what is bought most, one enjoys what most enjoy (cf. GSZ 35).

> In the behavior of everyday life, the rule-like pushes itself forward. The demand to do something that everyone does, not to attract attention, brings an all-absorbing type to dominance that is comparable on a new level to that of the most primitive times ... The individual is dissolved in function. To be is to be objective; where personality would be palpable, objectivity would be broken through. (GSZ 43)

Already in this early work, Jaspers' liberal ethos of humanity forms the background for the critique of mass society. The human right to individual self-realization in the greatest possible freedom and personal responsibility for one's own deviant life-plan must be preserved in modern industrial society.

The book is not a-political because it contains political reflections. The range of those reflections goes from reflections on state consciousness (GSZ 79–86), peace policy (GSZ 86–91), methods of political actions (GSZ 91–94) to the role of education for the state (GSZ 98–114). The phenomenon of power and the state's monopoly on power are also topics of critical reflection. Jaspers speaks out against the installation of a professional army in Germany. He fears that this would bring about a danger of political monopolization of power and ultimately the danger of establishing a dictatorial system of rule (cf. GSZ 89).

9.3 Dealing with the Guilt of the Germans for National Socialism

The book DIE SCHULDFRAGE (THE QUESTION OF GUILT) reproduces parts of the series of lectures that Jaspers gave in the winter semester of 1945/1946 under the title "Die geistige Situation in Deutschland" (The Intellectual Situation in Germany). Among the audience were many students who had just returned home from the lost war at the newly opened Heidelberg University. That Jaspers played a significant role in the organizational development and intellectual renewal of the university after the end of the war is made clear by Oliver Immel in his introduction to the

university writings in the Jaspers-Collected Works Edition.[3] Jaspers himself wrote
about his intention with the book in the afterword of the edition in 1962:

> The Scripture was intended to serve self-reflection, to find the way to dignity in accepting
> the guilt that was clearly recognized in its nature. It also pointed to the complicity of the
> victorious powers, not to exonerate us, but for the sake of truthfulness, and also to quietly
> ward off possible self-righteousness, which in politics has disastrous consequences for all.
> That such a writing could be published under the occupation regime testifies to the freedom
> which this regime left to the spirit from the beginning. (Sch 85)

In this writing Jaspers demands a radical moral-political reversal in German politics
and in the minds of the German people as a whole. It can be pointedly said that in
doing so Jaspers advocated a "philosophy of political rebirth through existential
conversion in the political crisis".[4]

Jaspers also discusses a political event that was particularly topical at the time,
namely the Nürnberg Trial. This was conducted from 20th November 1945 to 1st
October 1946 against the main exponents (Jaspers speaks of "main war criminals")
of the Nazi regime. Jaspers provocatively refutes many of the misgivings circulating
in the German post-war public against this trial, such as: it was only a sham trial or
a show trial anyway, it meant an unjust and globally propagated "national disgrace"
for the entire German people. The trial proves a one-sided partiality of the war win-
ners against the loser Germany, etc. In contrast, Jaspers sees this trial as a first positive step "on the way to a world order." (Scheme 38) In contrast to all whitewashing
and suppression strategies regarding the crimes of the Nazi regime and the German
"Wehrmacht", he emphasizes:

> Germany committed numerous acts that (outside of any chivalry and against international
> law) led to the extermination of populations and other inhumanities. Hitler's actions were
> against any possibility of reconciliation from the start. There was only victory or downfall.
> Now the consequences of doom are here. Every demand for chivalry is – even where
> numerous individual soldiers and whole units of troops are free of guilt and for their part
> have always behaved in a chivalrous manner – invalid where the Wehrmacht as an organiza-
> tion has taken over to carry out Hitler's criminal orders. (Sch 34)

An important theme in this work is the confrontation with the sweeping collective
guilt thesis that was propagated at the time by Sigrid Undset, who later won the
Norwegian Nobel Prize for Literature. In an essay on the "re-education of the
Germans", she accused all German citizens of being guilty for the rise and tyranny
of the National Socialists. Jaspers counters this accusation with differentiating considerations about different shares of guilt, responsibilities, liabilities, and necessary
punishments of individual Germans. He distinguishes between four concepts of
guilt, which he links to concrete political demands on the population of post-war

---

[3] Cf. Oliver Immel, Einleitung des Herausgebers. In: ders. (ed.), *Karl Jaspers – Schriften zur
Universitätsidee.* In: *Karl Jaspers Gesamtausgabe*, Vol. I/21, Basel 2016, XXXI–XXXVI.
[4] Cf. Werner Schneiders, *Karl Jaspers in der Kritik,* Bonn 1967, 126.

Germany. The Heidelberg historian *Reinhard Koselleck* later regretted the lack of resonance of Jaspers' writing in the inner-German political discussion of the time:

> What he formulated in 1945 on the question of guilt – against the thesis of collective guilt – was hardly received at the time in its sober weighing of exoneration and burden. The distinction between criminal and moral guilt, between political liability and metaphysical responsibility – these distinctions seemed out of touch in the dense fog of German larmoyant self-exculpations and self-accusations – but they potentially offered a clear framework of judicial norms of action.[5]

Jaspers differentiates the concept of guilt by distinguishing the following types of guilt:

(a) *Criminal guilt* concerns all Germans who committed crimes during the Nazi era; they must be punished and judged ruthlessly by the courts of the victorious powers and by a newly established German judiciary.

> Not every German, even only a very small minority of Germans, has to suffer punishment for crimes, another minority has to atone for National Socialist activities. One may defend oneself. The courts of the victors or the German instances set up by them judge. (Sch 49)

(b) The *political guilt* concerns all citizens of the Nazi state, because they enabled or did not prevent the establishment of this state or its temporary functioning. When the Nazi elites committed crimes in the name of the German state, they always did so in the name of all those who were members of that state after the National Socialists seized power in 1933. For Jaspers, this implies not only a collective political joint liability of all citizens for the damage caused by the Nazi state, but also responsibility for material reparations. Reparations must be paid to the survivors of the Holocaust and to all states attacked by National Socialist Germany. In addition, the new borders of Germany established by the victorious powers must be unconditionally recognized. This applies above all the recognition of the Oder-Neisse line on the eastern border.

> Everyone acts politically in the modern state, at least when voting in elections or by refraining from voting. (Sch 41)

(c) *Moral guilt*, unlike political guilt, can only be attributed to individuals. It results from such complex psychological phenomena as comfortable self-deception about the goals and inhumane rule practices of the Nazi regime, from the unconditionality of a blind, German-national outlook, and from partial approval of National Socialism. Even occasional "inner alignment" and "fellow-travelling" with the existing Nazi system entails moral guilt. That Jaspers endeavored to differentiate even further is evidenced by the following statement about party membership in the NSDAP (National Socialist German Worker Party).

---

[5] Reinhard Koselleck, Jaspers, die Geschichte und das Überpolitische. In: Jeanne Hersch et al. (eds.), *Karl Jaspers. Philosoph – Arzt – politischer Denker,* München, Zurich 1986, 293.

> It is decisive for the sense of going along in what context and for what motives someone became a party member. Every year and every situation has its peculiar excuses and peculiar burdens, which can only be distinguished in each individual case. (Sch 48)

The decisive point here is that only the German people themselves and each individual German have to decide on the respective moral guilt in an effortful process of reflection. This guilt cannot be erased by punishments and reparation treaties, but also not by servile and undignified confessions of guilt towards the victorious powers. Blanket moral condemnations from a "judge's seat in the world", no matter who they come from, need not be accepted.

Jaspers connects the demand for a process of reflection with the idea that an "inner moral conversion" (Scheme 16) should be brought about in each individual. According to his conception of human dignity, this conversion must take place on one's own initiative and not as a result of pressure from outside. This reflects a notion already discussed in Chap. 3 with the becoming of the self in borderline situations. Jaspers saw in the Nazi era a kind of political and moral borderline situation that could not be overcome by superficial strategies of repression. It had to be dealt with through an honest process of self-reflection. In doing so, it is necessary to become aware of the historical, social, economic and psychological preconditions for the development of the Nazi movement in Germany. This process of reflection, which each individual must undertake by examining his or her own share of guilt, should be accompanied by a process of public discussion and enlightenment. This is a necessary condition for the moral and political "transformation" of the German people after the catastrophe of National Socialism. Moral guilt would have to be combined with a sense of guilt and remorse and – resulting from this – a new and expanded worldview.

(d) Jaspers sees a *metaphysical guilt* where the "solidarity with man as man" is lost, "if I survive where the other is killed." (Scheme 48)[6] At first glance, one might object that this concept of guilt is very vague, and it has also been argued against it that it strongly overlaps with the concept of moral guilt and is therefore superfluous. A theological interpretation has also been suggested,[7] because Jaspers makes statements that refer to God, for example, when he speaks of a "transformation of human self-consciousness before God" as a consequence of metaphysical guilt (cf. Scheme 21).

If one interprets metaphysical guilt as a lack of absolute solidarity with all human beings, the following question arises: How can one be in absolute solidarity with all people, if in existential communication one is supposed to be in absolute solidarity only with the communication partner(s)? Doesn't the existential relationship, which is concentrated on only one person and whose exclusivity Jaspers emphasizes, exclude all other people from the start? *Dominic*

---

[6] Cf. Dominic Kaegi, Was ist metaphysische Schuld? In: *Jb. der Österreichischen Karl-Jaspers-Gesellschaft*, Jg. 14 (2001), 9–39; cf. also: Alan M. Olson, Metaphysical Guilt. In: *Jb. der Österreichischen Karl-Jaspers-Gesellschaft, Jg.* 26 (2013), 167–190.

[7] Cf. Ralf Kadereit, *Karl Jaspers und die Bundesrepublik Deutschland. Politische Gedanken eines Philosophen,* Paderborn, München 1999, 32.

Kaegi, who has drawn attention to this problem, therefore suggests that the notion of metaphysical guilt should "be read as a self-critique of the narrowing of existential communication."[8]

Another interpretation could also be the following: In the case of existential communication with a fellow human being, it is a matter of a subjective experience that is characterized by momentary character as well as experience of existential freedom and reference to transcendence. Due to its subjective depth of this experience it transcends the objective time frame. In the case of absolute solidarity in connection with metaphysical guilt, on the other hand, the focus is on an ideal of responsibility whose realization does not fall outside the objective time frame in the existential sense.

The idea of guilt is based here on the universally valid insight into the human condition. It is undeniable that being human is necessarily connected with negative forms of experience that are the same for all human beings: every person is a living being susceptible to suffering and pain, subject to the aging process, and whose life inevitably ends with death. The human being is always confronted with the antinomian basic structure of being, which makes him experiencing failures (moments of foundering) in many ways. From the insight into the basic structure of human existence, which is common to all human beings, solidarity with all human beings can be derived. One can also see this solidarity as the basis for the acceptance of universally valid human rights.

Incidentally, a similar thought can be found in a contemporary of Jaspers, namely *Albert Camus.* Like Jaspers, he too was seen as a continuator of the tradition of the French moralists. In his second major philosophical work, DER MENSCH IN DER REVOLTE starts from the consideration that there is a "nature common to all men".

All human beings have in common both, the striving for the absolute and unity at one hand, and the experience of failure (foundering), as well as the inevitability of death on the other. For this reason, there is a "complicity" or "community of destiny of all human beings."[9] Everybody is confronted with the strangeness and irrationality of the world, the failure of absolute claims to meaning, and the problem of death. Individual loneliness and the nihilistic emptiness of meaning can only be countered by becoming aware of community with others and by "solidarity" with the failure and suffering of fellow human beings. Mutual recognition of a common destiny creates connections with one another. They must come together "in the only value that could save them from nihilism: the complicity of people wrestling with their fate."[10]

---

[8] Dominic Kaegi, What is Metaphysical Guilt? In: *Jb. der Österreichischen Karl-Jaspers-Gesellschaft,* Jg. 14 (2001), 9.

[9] Albert Camus, *Der Mensch in der Revolte,* Reinbek 1980, 227.

[10] Ibid., 230.

9.4   The Political-Moral Background of Reflections on History After 1945

When Jaspers published his book VOM URSPRUNG UND ZIEL DER GESCHICHTE (ON THE ORIGIN AND GOAL OF HISTORY) in 1948, the world political situation was still determined by the "Cold War" between the Soviet Union and the USA. It could not be ruled out that a war would break out between the two superpowers. Therefore, Jaspers was concerned at the time with the question of whether a permanent state of world peace was even possible. He comes to a rather pessimistic conclusion:

> The limit of historical possibilities has its deep ground in being human. A completed final state can never be reached in the human world, because man is a being that constantly pushes beyond itself, is not only unfinished, but incomplete. (UZG 199)

Even if a permanent state of world peace can never be achieved, at least a world peace order can be striven for as a political goal, but only on the basis of a pluralistic-democratic social order. In view of the world political hegemonic aspirations of the Stalinist Soviet Union at that time, Jaspers warns against a "totalitarian world empire" and pleads for a federalist world order (cf. UZG 184–188). In this context, he again criticizes totalitarian, political ways of thinking, which suggest that political options for action, economic structures and social relations can be planned rationally in their entirety and down to the last detail (cf. UZG 171–181).

The confrontation of the "Western world" with the Eastern bloc states at that time was the reason why Jaspers dealt more closely with socialism. He distinguishes between two fundamentally different socialist currents: the most welcome current is liberal, democratic socialism, whose "origin is the idea of freedom and justice for all" (cf. UZG 171–178). For Jaspers, it constitutes a basic tendency of the age of modernity, with which distributive justice is associated as a condition of freedom. In this sense, "almost everyone today is a socialist" (UZG 162). Presumably, Jaspers' positive understanding of socialism was influenced by the discussion about a "free socialism" that was conducted among Heidelberg intellectuals after the end of the war. At the end of 1946, *Alfred Weber* and *Dolf Sternberger,* among others, who together with Jaspers published the journal *"Die Wandlung",* founded an "Action Group Heidelberg on Democracy and Free Socialism". *Alexander Mitscherlich* and *Alfred Weber* published a programmatic paper of this group under the title "Free Socialism".[11]

For Jaspers, the socialist current to be rejected is "Marxist socialism", "Marxism" or "communism", in which he also sees a basic tendency of the age. At the time, it served the Soviet Union and the Eastern Bloc states to legitimize the totalitarian, state exercise of power in their sphere of influence. In a pointed passage, Jaspers contrasts the two socialist currents:

> Socialism, which as communism, in enthusiasm for the certain salvation of mankind, takes the shaping of the future in total planning by force into its own hands, and socialism as the

---

[11] Cf. Alexander Mitscherlich, Alfred Weber, *Freier Sozialismus*, Heidelberg 1946.

idea of gradual realization in the coexistence of a free democracy are alien to each other. The first consumes man who surrenders to it in a faith appearing as science, and the non-believers as an available material of violence. The second does not charm, lives presently, needs the sobriety of reason and the humanity of incessant communication. (UZG 176)

9.5   Concern for the Future of Man in the "Cold War" Phase of the Atomic Bomb Age

When Jaspers published the book DIE ATOMBOMBE UND DIE ZUKUNFT DES MENSCHEN (THE ATOMIC BOMB AND THE FUTURE OF MAN) in 1958, the world political constellation was still dominated by the "Cold War". Both superpowers of the twentieth century, the Soviet Union and the USA (Jaspers speaks incorrectly of Russia and America) were striving for hegemony in world politics. Jaspers saw the possession of the hydrogen atomic bomb by both superpowers as a tremendous danger to being human in general. He responds to the now existing possibility of humanity's self-annihilation by transferring the concept of the borderline situation to the political world situation of the time. Whereas in the period of existential philosophy before the Second World War this term served as a subjective category of experience to designate individual, existential borderline experiences. In the atom bomb-book it becomes a designation for the situation of humanity as a whole. Mankind as such finds itself in a universal borderline situation characterized by two new kinds of danger: the danger that the technical development of control instruments and surveillance apparatuses in totalitarian political systems such as the Soviet Union will prevent any individual conduct of life in freedom and personal responsibility. A second danger is the fact that the technical development of the atomic bomb will make the annihilation of the entire human race through nuclear war possible.

Jaspers wanted to raise the universal, political borderline situation to the general consciousness and to think about possible ways out.

> The fact that the catastrophe is constantly before our eyes as a possibility, even a probability, is today a tremendous chance for self-reflection in general and at the same time the only chance for political renewal and thus for warding off the catastrophe. (AZM 24)

In analyzing the balance of power in world politics at that time, Jaspers comes to the conclusion that with Soviet Russian totalitarianism the existence of pluralistic-liberal social systems is at stake. Only in the Western, parliamentary democracies, he argues, is it possible to lead a self-determined life in freedom and open communication with other people. Looking back on the rise of the totalitarian Nazi regime, Jaspers warns against compromising with Soviet totalitarianism and underestimating its expansionist tendencies. Thus, the formula of "political coexistence" or "peaceful coexistence" (cf. AZM 150–152), which *Nikita Khrushchev* had decreed as the Soviet Union's new foreign policy doctrine at the XXth Party Congress of the CPSU on 25 February 1956, was useful for the moment in preventing a war between the two superpowers. On closer examination, however, this formula is dangerous for the democratic states because the intellectual confrontation (the "ideological strug-gle") between the totalitarian Marxist worldview and the liberal-democratic world outlook is possible only in the open democracies. Here the ideological propaganda and indoctrination strategies of the Marxist ideologists have an advantage, because the ideology of Marxism-Leninism can be presented in public in the Western democracies, while the open ideological discussion is not possible in the Soviet Union and the other states of the real existing socialism. There, critical expressions of opinion would be suppressed from the outset by the state censorship apparatus. Marxist political and ideological positions would simply be decreed as the only valid ones by the ideological propaganda headquarters of the CPSU (and its chief ideologist *Mikhail Suslov*) without public discussion.

> The spiritual struggle of the totalitarian on the soil of the free world is dangerous for the free world because of the motives that everywhere meet the totalitarian. It works the magic of a paradise, which, however, only exists as long as one does not live in it oneself, but has one's dreams fulfilled through imaginations and through given promises: ...In the sense in which Marx conceived of religion as opium for the people, he himself created a new opium. (AZM 165)

On the then current, political discussion about a neutralization of Germany, Jaspers takes the following position: The principle of political neutrality can only be consid-ered positive if a state invokes it, which has no claim to expand its power and makes the greatest possible effort for military self-defense (cf. AZM 189). An example of this for Jaspers was Switzerland. For Germany this principle is not applicable. A status of neutrality is to be rejected because Germany, due to its size and geographi-cal position in the middle of Europe, it would be necessarily at the center of the political confrontation of the great powers.

> It is true that neutrality of a territory can be advantageous for both opponents. But neutrality would only be credible with a power that can defend itself. A de facto neutrality of a reunited Germany would be impossible. It would only be a matter of demilitarization, leav-ing the country at the mercy of whoever could get there fastest in the event of war. (AZM 188)

In view of the danger of nuclear war at that time, Jaspers reflects on the possibilities and conditions of a political state of world peace. Among other things, he gives thought to the nature of a confederation of states as opposed to a centralized world state, referring in some arguments to *Kant's* writing ZUM EWIGEN FRIEDEN. He also considered the successful, non-violent peace strategy of *Mahatma Gandhi*. He rela-tivizes it, however, because this strategy could have only been successful under the framework conditions of a basically liberal-democratic colonial power (Great Britain) (cf. AZM 64–69).

9.6   The Provocative Statement on the Doctrine of German Reunification

Jaspers had a political conversation with the journalist *Thilo Koch* on 10 August 1960 on television, which was published the same year under the title FREIHEIT UND WIEDERVEREINIGUNG. ÜBER AUFGABEN DEUTSCHER POLITIK. (FREEDOM AND REUNIFICATION. ABOUT TASKS OF GERMAN POLITICS). He started the conversation by arguing that there were three urgent political tasks for German politics. The urgent one concerns the survival of mankind: the realization of the "idea of world peace in freedom through a world confederation not fixed by states" (FW 13). The second task concerns the "self-assertion of the Occident and the development of freedom" against the danger of "total domination". Referring to the Federal Republic of Germany (FRG), he formulates as the third important task the realization of a German state which has "its place in the whole of the Occident" and could serve as an example for the development of free, democratic styles of life (cf. FW 13).

In the aforementioned interview and in newspaper articles, Jaspers opposed the political doctrine that was at his days part of the basic consensus of all democratic, political parties in the Federal Republic: namely, the doctrine of the reunification of Germany, which was then also a component of the Basic Law. Jaspers argues against this doctrine by portraying the demand for reunification as an outdated relic of Bismarck's nation-state thinking in Germany. This, he argues, ultimately led to the catastrophe of Hitler's National Socialist regime. Therefore, the demand for a national unity is not only outdated, but under the given power-political conditions not realizable, even peace-endangering. The Federal Republic of Germany should renounce this doctrine and officially recognize the Marxist German Democratic Republic (GDR) as the second German state. The goal of German foreign policy should not be reunification, but the effort to gain freedom for the GDR-citizens in their repressive state.

> And I don't think there is any sense at all today in what made sense in the 19th century and once meant a great opportunity that was squandered by Hitler's Reich. Now that that is over, there is no longer any sense in propagating German unity; there is only a sense in wishing for our countrymen to be free. (FW 111)

By turning away from the doctrine of reunification, Jaspers hoped that both interpersonal contacts between the Germans of the two states could be improved and the scope of freedom of the citizen(s) in the GDR could be expanded within the framework of the Eastern bloc. With the existential-philosophical assumption in the background that genuine communication is only possible between equal partners, he pleaded for the recognition of the GDR's statehood. He proposed the granting of economic aid and offering of friendship to the representatives of "Eastern Germany" and hoped in this way to strengthen the GDR's self-confidence as a state in its own right.

He opposed also to realize a sort of national unity through the reunification of the two German states because he himself preferred for both parts of Germany a position within a "confederal unity of Europe". This superior unity would make the doctrine of reunification superfluous.

> The unity that matters today is the confederal unity of Europe and of Europe with America. Whether in this great unity, which is indispensable for the self-assertion of all free states, one or more German states are confederative or neutralizing members, is irrelevant to the common destiny. (FW 17)

The then Chairman of the Council of State of the GDR and head of the dominant party SED, *Walter Ulbricht,* who was about to initiate an exchange of views between the SED-party and the SPD-party in Western Germany, wrote Jaspers a personal letter. There he praised Jaspers' suggestion of a dialogue between the two German states. Jaspers then distanced himself from "false friends", but maintained the demand for such a dialogue (cf. Ant 151–167).

No less provocative in view of the activities of the associations of expellees in the FRG was the explicit call to German politicians of all parties to unconditionally recognize the Oder-Neisse-line as the final eastern border vis-à-vis Poland (cf. FW 34–35).

A domestic issue that Jaspers also took up and criticized at the time was the enactment of the Basic Law for the new democratic German state, the Federal Republic. Jaspers saw the Basic Law as merely provisional, because it did not come into being on the basis of discussion by a broad majority of the population. The law was enacted "from above", so that the grassroots, i.e. the people, could not participate in the discussion and identify with the law.

> Thus, the ... Basic Law was not a democratically grown structure originating from the people and based on the prerequisites in the thinking of the population. It was not directly imposed by the victors, but written by Germans on their instructions in forms of democratic legality ... A transformation of the political spirit had not taken place. Instead of a new creation from the democratic idea, the program of the restoration of German unity took its place. (FW 61)

9.7   Public Statement on the Domestic Debate on the Statute of Limitation of Punishments for Nazi Crimes (1965)

On the occasion of the debates in the Bundestag on 10 and 25 March 1965, about the abolition of the time limit for the conviction of Nazi crimes, Jaspers gave an interview to the editor-in-chief *Rudolf Augstein* for the well-known weekly magazine "Der Spiegel". This interview appeared under the title "There is no statute of limitations for genocide". One year later it was also published in the book WOHIN TREIBT DIE BUNDESREPUBLIK? (WHERE IS THE FEDERAL REPUBLIC DRIFTING? or THE FUTURE OF GERMANY). As it can already be seen from the title of the interview, Jaspers was firmly against the decision to impose a statute of limitations on Nazi crimes. In the parliamentary decision, the statute of limitations was not lifted, but only extended by four years. Jaspers was deeply indignant and analyzes the parliamentary debate and the speeches of representatives on the basis of the parliamentary minutes. He then criticizes representatives by name who had spoken approvingly on the issue in the parliament. He accuses them of lacking intellectual and moral-political culture because they had made the statute of limitations to a purely legal, juridical question instead of conceiving it as an immensely political and moral question. (BR 71–73).

As the political scientist *Kurt Sontheimer pointed out* in a commentary on a new edition of WOHIN TREIBT DIE BUNDESREPUBLIK? (1988),[12] for Jaspers the behavior of politicians in the statute of limitations debate was both an indication of the extent to which politicians had distanced themselves from Nazi-era modes of behavior and thought, and the extent to which the moral-political conversion to a genuine, democratic form of government in the FRG had actually succeeded. One can rightly assume that all of Jaspers' statements on German domestic and foreign policy after 1945 were guided by the deep conviction that a radical reversal of the way of thinking in the political culture of the FRG was required in order for a truly new, democratic state to emerge after the Nazi dictatorship.

9.8   Massive Criticism of Political Conditions in the Federal Republic of Germany (1966)

From Jaspers' point of view, the desired reversal of the political culture in the Federal Republic of Germany had not taken place. He points out that the break with the "National Socialist criminal state" was not radical enough, because, for example, in the judiciary of the new German state, people hold public office who were involved in the inhuman jurisdiction of the Nazi regime. Jaspers now also accuses *Konrad Adenauer,* whom he had still praised as a "statesman of the Occident" (cf. FW 86–87), of having pursued an inconsistent denazification policy.

Moreover, Jaspers diagnoses a strong tendency towards a party oligarchy in the new, democratic state of the Federal Republic (cf. BR 130–140, 194–197). His polemic against the party state contains many arguments similar to those put forward by *Robert Michels* in his critique of the functionary elites in the party state.[13] As circumstantial evidence that a party elite focused on maintaining power increasingly excludes the people from the political process, Jaspers cites the following phenomena (cf. BR 127–139): The formation of a coalition of major parties, state party financing, the five-percent clause, whereby smaller political groups are excluded from political decision-making processes, the election of the Federal President not by the people but by the Federal Assembly, party protectionism at the allocation of state posts, arbitrary, undemocratic selection of candidates for political positions via the parties' electoral lists, lack of efficiency of parliamentary control

---

[12] Cf. Kurt Sontheimer, *Einführung zur Neuausgabe von "Wohin treibt die Bundesrepublik?",* München, Zurich 1988, II–IV.

[13] Cf. Robert Michels, *Zur Soziologie des Parteiwesens in der modernen Demokratie,* Leipzig 1911.

in the case of political scandals, and the "people-dumbing advertising" before elections.

9.9   Last Reaction to Criticism of His Critique of German Policy (1967)

In the last political writing that Jaspers published two years before his death as ANTWORT. ZUR KRITIK MEINER SCHRIFT "WOHIN TREIBT DIE BUNDESREPUBLIK?", not only the domestic political but also the foreign political perspective is present. The moral-political concern of moral-political conversion in German politics forms the starting point for massive criticism of the political parties and politicians in the Federal Republic of Germany. Thus, Jaspers denounces the fact that in the CDU-SPD coalition government formed in 1966 *(Kiesinger-Brandt)*, *Kurt Georg Kiesinger*, a former NSDAP member, was elected Chancellor. (Antw 214–221).

Jaspers also polemicized against the formation of the Grand Coalition between the CDU and the SPD, seeing the end of democracy coming with its constitution. He was firmly convinced that a democratic form of government must always include a strong opposition party in addition to a governing party.

> Today we are faced with the question of what the grand coalition will do from its absolute power, unrestricted by any opposition. It can do what it wants. (Antw 214)

To the proponents of emergency laws, Jaspers counters:

> All these decent and well-meaning people, but miserable politicians do not know and do not carry in their hearts what political freedom is, they want only one thing: security. In my book I wrote: The blind urge for security wants the impossible: absolute security. By wrong security measures he destroys just the possible security. Those who want security by the wrong means plunge into ruin through security fanaticism. (Antw 111–112)

The Emergency Laws were passed by the German Bundestag on 30 May 1968. This triggered strong protests by the so-called extra-parliamentary opposition (APO). These laws added an emergency constitution to the Basic Law, which was supposed to secure the state's ability to act in crisis situations (natural disaster, uprising, war).

Concerning German foreign policy, Jaspers deals with the relations of the Federal Republic of Germany at that time with Russia, the USA, China and de Gaulle's France. He comes to the conclusion that the Federal Republic should enter into close ties with the USA (cf. Antw 15–61).

If, from today's perspective, Jaspers was wrong in his view that there could be no non-violent reunification of Germany and that one must therefore resign oneself to the division of Germany. The reason for this opinion may be found in the world political situation at the time. The fact that the non-violent reunification of the two German states took place more than twenty years after Jaspers' death may be seen as a confirmation of his historical-philosophical assumption, that the future is "open" and non-forecastable.

The statement that a dictatorship could not be revolutionized non-violently from within was also wrong. Jaspers formulated this thesis apodictically due to the shock experience with the Nazi dictatorship:

> Once the dictatorship is there, liberation from within is impossible. (Sch 68)

Jaspers held to this assumption throughout his life. That it was false in its general validity-claim was shown more than twenty years after Jaspers' death not only by the non-violent revolution in the former GDR, but also earlier by the non-violent removal of military dictatorships and the restoration of democratic social orders in European countries such as Spain (1975–1978), Greece (1974) and Portugal (1976).

Political Philosopher or Merely Political Writer?

10

10.1 The Dissention Concerning the Term "Political Philosopher"

In his last political writings Jaspers caused a misunderstanding because he wanted to be understood there merely as a "political writer". This provoked many a derogatory judgement about his political thinking. However, if one analyses the context of these statements more closely, one comes to the conclusion that Jaspers does not use the word "writer" in the meaning that is familiar from everyday usage and from literary theory. There, persons are called writers who write novels, stories, essays, etc. In so doing they create from their literary imagination ideal-typical fictitious persons as patterns of identification and as symbols of human destinies and typical modes of behavior. Jaspers, on the other hand, used the word "writer" for political thinkers who "glimpse" and "think through" the "horizons of political possibilities. They consider in "effectual imagination …in the space of possibilities the horizons of political worldviews." In this way, they enable the active politician to "orient himself in the broad space of conceivabilities" without being able to derive his political resolutions and decisions directly from them (cf. HS 366–371). That Jaspers uses "political writer" synonymously with "political thinker" or "political theorist," in explicit contrast to persons who are actively engaged as politicians, is evidenced by the following passage from the preface of his book WOHIN TREIBT DIE BUNDESREPUBLIK?:

> The writer may set the highest standards and think through designs consistently. The statesman must take the path in reality and seize the means which seem to him possible and effective under the guidance of his basic political conception. Before the mighty stream of history the writer stands only as on the shore. Thus I also stand before the political work in the Federal Republic, which is done by many active people with the use of their powers, with the respect of an inactive person, even though I so often cannot agree, expose actions, speeches, plans, and persons to criticism. (BR 13)

A number of skeptical questions have been raised about Jaspers' understanding of politics:

© Springer-Verlag GmbH Germany, part of Springer Nature 2022
K. Salamun, *Karl Jaspers*, https://doi.org/10.1007/978-3-476-05896-6_10

- Can Jaspers be called a political philosopher at all, or is he after all only a writer who acquired knowledge about politics from newspapers and magazines and then took a public stand on current political issues?
- Was he politically naive because he had no sense of political normality and appeals to political reversals only that are at best appropriate for exceptional situations in politics?[1]
- Was Jaspers, in ignorance of political normality, not making far too high moral demands on politics with his call for a reversal from the old to a new, reason-guided politics?
- Don't such demands make the discrepancy between the moral claims and the actual behavior of people involved in politics feel all the greater and more disillusioning?
- Doesn't Jaspers remain caught up in overly romantic categories about political thought and action?
- Was he at all a political philosopher who expressed generalities or at least concerns about the phenomenon of politics?

These argumentations can be countered by some of the following reflections.

10.2   As Political Philosopher Pointing to the Normative-Moral Dimension of Politics

Jaspers was undoubtedly a political philosopher, because in his philosophy he developed thoughts that are of importance for politics and political science. For the latter, however, only if it is not understood exclusively as a science of facts that uses strict empirical-rational methods. However, as soon as the normative dimension of the political is at stake, as soon as goals for political action or value standards for political education are at stake, empirical evidence of facts in political processes, actions and institutions is not sufficient. Then it is always a question of political-moral value-attitudes that underlie political action. These include those moral and liberal-democratic attitudes that characterize Jaspers' liberal ethos of humanity.

It would be wrong to identify the liberal political philosopher Jaspers with the variant of liberalism that has been painted on the wall in the Anglo-Saxon liberalism-communitarianism debate. There, representatives of the social-philosophical current of thought of communitarianism have claimed that a liberal position would necessarily dissolve all ties to traditions and traditional community values.

---

[1] Cf. Klaus von Beyme, Karl Jaspers – Vom philosophischen Außenseiter zum *Praeceptor Germaniae*. In: *Heidelberg 1945*, ed. by Jürgen C. Heß, Hartmut Lehmann and Volker Sellin in conjunction with Detlev Junker and Eike Wolgast, Stuttgart 1996, 147.

Liberalism stylizes an unbound, free-floating Ego, which in its self-realization is completely free of ties to traditional values.[2]

In Jaspers' case, there are ties to liberal, moral values from the occidental, western liberal tradition, which preclude the isolation and absolutization of the self. Namely truthfulness, responsibility, willingness to communicate and dialogue, openness to encounters with different cultures, etc.

If one wants to summarize two controversial assessments of Jaspers' political philosophy in two opposing theses, the following picture would emerge:

Thesis 1: The attempt to introduce an ethos of humanity into politics is unrealistic and ultimately counterproductive. Politics is not about following or not following high moral principles, but about pragmatically solving political factual problems: such as balancing the interests of competing claims of different social groups, balancing claims to power of political parties, etc. If politics is moralized, as Jaspers intended, this leads to the fanatization of political disputes and opens up the possibility of morally discrediting political competitors in public. The extent to which the moralization of politics can interfere with the real business of politics has often been evident from public debates about the moral integrity of presidents and top politicians in the United States. (e.g. the Bill Clinton-Monica Lewinsky affair). Therefore, viewpoints that link politics with morality should be rejected. Discussions about morality are an integrative factor in modern, de-ideologized society,[3] but an actual moralization of politics is by no means desirable. This leads to an inability to compromise and to the misuse of morality for the purpose of disavowing political competitors in the service of one's own interests in gaining or maintaining power. Put even more pointedly, one could argue that moralizing politics opens the door to a despicable investigative and sensational journalism. The latter is not seriously interested in constructive democratic control of political events. Its primary interest is to "finish off" even serious and talented politicians in the public eye by sensationalizing news about their moral misconduct. The primary goal is to increase the circulation figures of trivial-populist magazines and weeklies.

Thesis 2: The attempt to introduce an ethos of humanity into politics is a most welcome and necessary undertaking. For politics is not only politics of interests, power and facts, as it may appear from the pragmatic perspective of "Realpolitikern" and positivist political scientists. Political action is not the sole result of scientific-technical factual considerations and situation analyses, but always implies value decisions. This was explicitly emphasized last least by *Max Weber*, despite or precisely because of his realist understanding of politics. The

---

[2] Cf. Rainer Forst, Kommunitarismus und Liberalismus – Stationen einer Debatte. In: Axel Honneth (ed.), *Kommunitarismus. Eine Debatte über die moralischen Grundlagen moderner Gesellschaften*, Frankfurt, New York 1993, 181–212; Will Kymlicka, Das freischwebende Ich. In: ders, *Politische Philosophie heute*, Frankfurt, New York 1997, 176–184.

[3] Cf. Werner Becker, Der fernethische Illusionismus und die Realität. In: Kurt Salamun (ed.), *Aufklärungsperspektiven. Weltanschauungsanalyse und Ideologiekritik*, Tübingen 1989, 1–8.

humane standards for political value decisions must always be reconsidered and publicly demanded, otherwise political action degenerates into egoistic unscrupulousness and the exaltation of an inhumane efficiency ideology. In Jaspers, one can see an excellent example of a thinker who did not trivialize or ignore the value and humanity dimension of the political, but rather accentuated it to a special degree.

The Idea of Democracy, Reason and Politics

11

11.1 Basic Principles of the Idea of Democracy

For Jaspers, the idea of democracy is an ideal of approximation that implies those basic principles that are regarded as necessary conditions for the existence of a pluralistic, liberal, parliamentary society. Those principles are:

the *principle of popular sovereignty*, i.e. the agreement that there may be no other form of legitimation of rule than that which emanates from the people; this principle implies the principle of universal, free, secret and equal suffrage (cf. AZM 42, 421, 429); further principles are: the principle of participation, according to which

> every citizen of the state is called upon to think and participate in politics and to share responsibility at some essential point which affects the whole. (AZM, 432);

the *principle of separation of powers and the rule of law*; the *majority principle*, insofar as it is associated with certain institutional protections for minorities;

the *principle of plurality of parties and interest groups*; the *principle of critical publicity* (cf. AZM 43) and institutionalized control of holders of power, be they holders of political, economic or other positions of power;

the *principle of the greatest possible conformity of the constitution (the constitutional norms) with constitutional reality*;

the *principle of the welfare state*, at least to the extent that the innocently distressed, the sick and the socially weak are protected from total destitution by legally anchored social safety nets. That Jaspers did not ignore the social dimension of democracy is proven by the positive components of the idea of socialism that he emphasized (cf. AZM 217–219).

the *principle of the willingness to compromise and the balancing of interests* in disputes between social groups competing for life claims (such as ethnic groups) is also part of the idea of democracy.

© Springer-Verlag GmbH Germany, part of Springer Nature 2022
K. Salamun, *Karl Jaspers*, https://doi.org/10.1007/978-3-476-05896-6_11

That the realization of these principles can only be a gradual process and that democracy must not be propagated with a perfectionist claim as a finally attainable goal of salvation is clearly stated by Jaspers:

> Democracy is an idea. This means that it cannot be completed anywhere and that even as an ideal it eludes a vivid conception. Man, with his reason, sees the absence of a proper world arrangement to be brought to completion. The democratic idea corresponds to the consciousness of man's incompleteness. (AZM 425)

Without a *basic consensus* on the idea of democracy, there can be no democratic political system in the long term, be it presidential, plebiscitary or representative. This basic consensus is by no means self-evident. It must be constantly strengthened through political education and enlightenment and defended against anti-democratic political forces and ideas.

> In the idea of democracy, politics itself is education. But in contrast to the earlier politics and education, which were limited to privileged strata ... it is now a question of the education of the whole people ... All politics, which is not only skill for the moment, but foundation and continuation, continuity of effect, i.e. politics in the long run, is always at the same time also the education of a people. (AZM 447)

Even in societies that have experienced a radical change in their political system in the recent past and in which the transformation process from an authoritarian or totalitarian system of rule to a liberal, pluralistic-democratic system is still partly under way, it seems particularly important to carry out information and education work aimed at internalizing the idea of democracy in the consciousness and behavior of citizens. Deeply anchored mentality structures and attitudes from authoritarian times must be overhauled by elements of democratic ways of thinking in people's attitude and conviction systems. Incidentally, the well-known, political scientist *Kurt Sontheimer* also recognized that Jaspers' political thinking is significant for democratic culture. After he initially had criticized Jaspers harshly when his book WOHIN TREIBT DIE BUNDESREPUBLIK? (1966) was published, he appreciated Jaspers' political statements in the new edition (1988) of this book as follows:

> If you are looking for standards for the political culture of the Federal Republic, which is so much talked about and talked down today, you will find them in this book.[1]

11.2   Moral Values of a Reasonable Politics

The moral values that are constitutive for individual self-realization in borderline situations and existential communication for the existential philosopher Jaspers, mean the following if they are applied to politics by the political philosopher Jaspers: the new, reason-guided politics must be based on a considerable degree of

---

[1] Kurt Sontheimer, *Einführung zur Neuausgabe, Karl Jaspers, Wohin treibt die Bundesrepublik?* München, Zürich 1988, VII.

serenity and bravery for honestly assessing reality; it should be characterized by courage for autonomous self-reflection. The values that enable the individual human being in private life to bear and endure borderline situations with dignity should prevent those persons, who are acting politically in public life, from being carried away by blind emotional actions in crisis situations. They should also prevent people in a crisis situation from immediately clinging to the first possible way out without having thought through the consequences sufficiently. Jaspers' role model *Max Weber* also had these basic moral attitudes in mind in his reflections on politics in POLITIK ALS BERUF. (POLITICS AS A PROFESSION) There he emphasizes as desirable a type of politician who, in contrast to the "sterilely excited political dilettante", possesses "a sense of proportion" in political action and the ability,

> to let reality affect you with inner collection and calmness, i.e. the *distance* to things and people.[2]

The ability to distance oneself is understood by *Weber* also as the ability to distance oneself from oneself, i.e. from illusionary wishful thinking, self-deception and vanity, as well as from the pursuit of power for the purpose of "personal self-exhilaration."[3] The fact that the concept of the ability to distance oneself is, incidentally, also strongly morally impregnated in *Weber*. This becomes obvious by the close connection with the postulate of intellectual honesty.

For Jaspers, reason is to be transferred into the political action of the "new politics" because for him it is necessary connected with a fundamental readiness to accept responsibility: this is not only significant for the borderline situation of guilt, but it should play an important role in political decisions as a basic attitude of responsibility ethics,[4] as *Weber* demanded it in contrast to ethical fanaticism.

The moral values associated with the interpersonal communication ideal require the following behaviors when translated into a new policy:

* to take other people and peoples seriously and respect them in their peculiarities, characteristics and specific ways of life without prejudice;
* respect their ethnic, linguistic and cultural differences without prejudice;
* to recognize the principle of "level equality" or equal status of foreign groups in their development potential compared to ones own group;
* the effort to build up a basis of trust, both for the joint domestic solution of problems and for the solution of problems at the international, political level (cf. AZM 41).

From his conception of a new politics oriented towards reason, Jaspers formulates the following general principles for a political state of world peace (cf. AZM 40–46):

---

[2] Max Weber, *Politik als Beruf,* Berlin 5th. ed. 1968, 51.
[3] Ibid, 52.
[4] Ibid, 57–58.

- Unconditional recognition of "legality", i.e. adherence to concluded contracts. These are recognized as legally valid as long as they are not changed by new negotiations.
- Renunciation of absolute sovereignty and of the right to veto decisions of legally established bodies.

> The renunciation of absolute sovereignty and of the right of veto means the readiness to deal with the other "sovereigns" so reasonably and so credibly through constantly proving actions that a responsibility in reciprocity becomes perceptible and thereby a trust arises and grows. (AZM 41)

- Recognition of majority decisions of votes and elections. The latter must always be free and be secret elections (cf. AZM 42).
- The constitution, preservation and development of legal ties require unrestricted communication. There must be no restriction of the transmission of news, of intercourse between peoples and of public domestic and international discussion, i.e. no censorship of any kind (cf. AZM 43).

As far as the peacebuilding function of the UN (United Nations) and its organizational structure (the UN Charter) are concerned, Jaspers derives from his theoretical considerations the concrete demand to abolish the unanimity principle in the Security Council. This should make it no longer possible for a member to block peacebuilding measures (cf. ibid., 201–203). Jaspers is rather pessimistic about the UN's efforts so far to bring about a state of world peace on the basis of the concept of international law. He already sees serious deficiencies in the UN Charter. Although high demands and principles for peace-promoting measures are formulated there, the institutionalized institutions for intervention to maintain peace remain highly dubious and ineffective. Jaspers criticizes, among other things:

> A UN police force, consisting of the contingents of individual states, does not mean executive authority of the UN. For in fact each contingent remains under the supreme command of its state, which can recall it at any time. So it acts only as long as that state wants it to. Such a UN power has no combat power, but is only a symbol of the presence of the UN. (AZM 203)

Another accusation is directed against the instrumentalization of the UN for national interests:

> States that do not want the goals of the UN use the institution as a means of their politics. – For those who do not want and do not expect anything to be achieved by the grandly proclaimed goals of the UN, this institution has become a deliberately managed means of deception in the service of their own policies. (AZM 204)

11.3 Individuality and Democratic Politics

How strongly the liberal ideals of individual freedom, self-determination and personal responsibility are anchored in Jaspers' thinking is proven by his repeated warnings against closed political worldviews and totalitarian political systems. Such worldviews and systems block the freedom margins in which human beings can realize their individual and unjustifiable humanity in self-determination and personal responsibility. It depends on each individual to fight in politics against levelling tendencies in the "mechanized apparatus of mass existence" (GSZ 165), and to bring reason to bear in one's own life.

> Only in the individual man is the origin of the realization of reason. For every word he speaks, for every careless way of speaking about things, including political things, for every hasty judgment, every imprudence, he is just as responsible as for the absence of motives for freedom and solidarity with free men. (AZM 299)

How closely Jaspers links individualism with pluralist democracy is demonstrated by the following passage from his major work on political philosophy:

> Democracy is rather each individual himself. He has the responsibility for how he lives, what he thinks and works, what actions he decides to take, how he does all this in community with the other. To feel free of responsibility, that is the basic inversion of democracy. (AZM 439)

The basic individualistic component and the ideal of personal responsibility are also expressed in the idea of individual, reasonable statesmen. These are to be role models for the citizens in a democratic social order. In demarcation from collectivist conceptions of such a community, Jaspers emphasizes:

> But the community produced by reason is always first of all the community of individuals who find each other without contract, without organization, without expressing it, realizing the hidden solidarity of reason. (AZM 301)

With the idea of the reasonable statesman, Jaspers corrected his earlier view of political leadership in democratic social systems in the postwar writings. He always advocated the idea of political leadership by individual personalities of integrity of character. As exceptional personalities, politicians should be role models for the mass of the people and possess an authority accepted through trust.

In DIE GEISTIGE SITUATION DER ZEIT from 1931, the idea of the political leadership is closely linked to the critique of the tendencies towards anonymization and leveling in the technologized mass society. In this early writing, Jaspers, in the wake of romanticizing notions of "exceptional" personalities in *Nietzsche* ("free spirits") and following *Max Weber*'s idea of charismatic leadership, still advocated the political idea of the political leader in a way that is suitable to justify political decisionism. Thus Jaspers thinks there that at "the turning points of the order of existence, where the question is whether new creation or downfall," the decisive factor is that man "who from his own origin can seize the helm even against the masses." (GSZ 51).

After the experience of the misuse of the idea of the charismatic, political leadership in the Nazi ideology, Jaspers significantly modifies the earlier concept of political leadership. Henceforth he avoids the term "leader" and speaks only of the "responsible statesman" and the "politically acting human being." (cf. UZG 192–193). For the latter he postulates character traits that are similar in many aspects to those that *Max Weber* demanded for the profession of politics and which have already been mentioned above.

In DIE ATOMBOMBE UND DIE ZUKUNFT DES MENSCHEN, the new orientation towards the reasonable statesman is discussed in more detail and integrated into the context of the idea of a worldwide *"community of reasonable persons"*. This community, he argues, should pave the way for a new politics that promotes peace. The earlier, decisionist slant of the idea of political leadership is eliminated. The principle public character of all political action and the necessity of its permanent control and critical discussion by as many citizens as possible are now emphasized (cf. AZM 301–303, 326–339).

11.4   Totalitarian Ideological Tendencies in Political Thought

With "reason as a political mode of thought", Jaspers not only associates positive, democratic values, but also warns against anti-reason, anti-democratic modes of thought, which are booming in authoritarian and totalitarian ideologies. In doing so, Jaspers assumes a negative understanding of ideology by proposing the following definition:

> Ideology means a thought or imagination complex that presents itself to the thinker as absolute truth for the interpretation of the world and his situation in it, but in such a way that he thereby carries out a self-deception for justification, for concealment, for evasion, in some sense for his present advantage … The designation of a thought as ideology is the accusation of untruth and untruthfulness … (UZG 127).

For Jaspers, an anti-democratic, ideological tendency implies any attitude of thought that tends to dogmatize forms of knowledge and political principles by endowing them with a claim to absolute truth and exclusivity. The claim to be in the possession of an absolute truth, as it is raised by preachers of religious worldviews or by charismatic, political leaders, is based, in Jaspers' view, on an anti-democratic, elitist-authoritarian ideal of knowledge.

In contrast, he represents a democratic ideal of knowledge and cognition. The reasonable statesman must be a personality who sees himself as a representative and an educator of the people. A "communal public" in the sense of a critical public must be self-evident to him. He must not demand "unconditional trust" from the population, but should himself consciously challenge criticism (cf. AZM 334).

> Criticism should, as it were, examine, observe and question the politician who wants to become a statesman to see whether he is justified in taking the helm in this place. ... It must not tolerate blind or falsely motivated trust. ... The statesman should earn trust that is well-founded. He himself wants to win it in the storm of public opinion. His life is open because it concerns everyone. His being has a trait of the exemplary for a people who recognize themselves in him while remaining critical. (AZM 335)

For Jaspers, another anti-democratic, ideological tendency is immanent in every "totalistic way of thinking". Political doctrines with which it is pretended to want to plan societies or state structures as a whole or to control them as a whole are examples of this tendency. In revolutionary ideologies, the totalist claim expresses itself in the illusion that a social change is only meaningful if it is as total as possible and changes the existing conditions as a "whole".

Last but not least, Jaspers sees the totalistic, anti-democratic way of thinking in speculative systems of philosophy that claim to grasp the whole of reality. This refers to the presumptuous claim of philosophers to be able to combine the results of the natural sciences into a true, holistic and closed view of the world with a philosophical superscience (cf. RA 245–250). With the beginnings of modern science, the "scientific idea of totalism" (RA 246) found its way into the philosophy of classical rationalism. Jaspers cites *René Descartes* as an example. The latter contributed to a misconceived Enlightenment and to the superstition of science. The illusion that the progress of science and technology necessarily means progress "in the whole of being human" is a dangerous result of the totalistic way of thinking in the rationalist tradition.

In the tradition of German Idealism, this way of thinking has been particularly important in *Fichte and Hegel* and

> led to a dangerous increase of philosophical self-confidence ..., a supposed total knowledge that knows what God is and wants, and everywhere loses its amazement because it thinks itself in possession of the absolute truth. (UZG 131)

Jaspers also criticizes the totalistic form of thinking in connection with *Marx*'s deterministic theory of history. This pretends that there is a total insight into the development of history, which makes it possible to predict the future with certainty. A consequence of this illusion is a totalistic planning ideology, which wants to plan a society "as a whole". Attempts to realize this not only result in hypertrophic bureaucracies, but also in monopolies of power and totalitarian structures of rule that are incompatible with the idea of democracy. Traits of such a rule were ideally described by Jaspers in his remarks on totalitarianism in DIE ATOMBOMBE UND DIE ZUKUNFT DES MENSCHEN (cf. AZM 157–167).

Another anti-democratic, ideological tendency in Jaspers' sense is a monistic, closed mindset in politics. In contrast, he emphasizes the necessity of a pluralistic public sphere, plurality of opinions and parties, which are indispensable prerequisites for humane, democratic politics. Advocacy of plurality is a prerequisite for political freedom, which in turn is a prerequisite for existential freedom. The opposite tendency is to fixate on a "unity" and "cohesiveness" of political worldviews, groupings and parties. This leads all too easily to myopic and authoritarian party line thinking. In the criticism of the totalistic form of thinking and total planning ideologies cited here, Jaspers was influenced early on by other liberal thinkers, including *Alexis de Tocqueville*, *Walter Lippmann*, and *Friedrich von Hayek* (cf. UZG 178–180).

11.5   Reason, Politics and Universal Communication

For Jaspers, reason and communication cannot be separated. Reason can connect people,

> who can be extremely different in everything else, live and feel and want quite differently, it [reason] unites them more strongly than all difference separates them. (AZM 316)

The community of the reasonable must go "across all opposites, across denominations, across parties, across states" (AZM 309).

With the communicative function of reason, Jaspers aims at conveying an open-minded, open way of thinking, which he already discussed in his early thinking on the basis of the contrasting pair of categories "openness – closedness" (cf. PW 419–422). The open way of thinking is the antithesis of ways of thinking that pose a serious threat to the pluralistic, liberal constitutional state and democratic culture. Jaspers has in mind ethnocentric mindsets that perceive encounters with ethnically alien groups and different cultures as a threat. Such attitudes are reinforced by nationalist ideologies that see a fixation on the language, culture and way of life of one's own ethnic group as the only way to develop individual identities. From the perspective of communicative reason, as Jaspers suggests, encounters with foreign groups, cultures, and ways of life are welcome opportunities to enrich and differentiate one's own worldview and culture. One might well say, as *George Pepper* suggests in some of Jaspers' works,[5] that communicative reason, in Jaspers' sense, can form a basis for intercultural dialogue. Foreign cultures are respected in their peculiarities and their intrinsic value without having to deny or reveal one's own cultural origin because of it. Jaspers, too, despite all openness to other cultures, never made a secret of his own preference for the liberal-enlightenment culture of the Western Occident.

---

[5] Cf. George B. Pepper, Die Relevanz von Jaspers' Achsenzeit für interkulturelle Studien. In: Kurt Salamun (ed.), *Karl Jaspers. Zur Aktualität seines Denkens*, München 1991, 70–85.

On the Versatility of Jaspers' Thinking

12

12.1 Contributions to Several Fields of Philosophy

From the presentation of Jaspers' thought given here, it has become clear that Jaspers has left behind not only an extensive body of work, but also a body of work of great diversity. This will be briefly highlighted again here in summary from the point of view of disciplines of philosophy. When Jaspers is mentioned in many philosophy dictionaries together with *Heidegger* merely as one of the two main representatives of German existential philosophy, this truncated labeling obscures the view of the wealth of ideas of his philosophizing.

The fact that Jaspers was influenced by very different traditions and was therefore not always able to combine contradictory thought motifs without breaks or contradictions may also contribute to the truncated view of his philosophy. The most important traditions from which he adopted thought motifs are:

- the tradition of European Enlightenment philosophy and political liberalism, which flowed into his philosophy via *Kant* as an Enlightenment philosopher and via the thinking of *Max Weber*;
- the tradition of the critique of rationalism which he found in the writings of *Nietzsche, Kierkegaard and Weber*; and finally
- the tradition of speculative metaphysics of being, with which he became familiar through the works of *Plato, Plotinus, Hegel and Schelling*.

From the perspective of analytical philosophy in the tradition of neopositivism, Jaspers has been accused of basing his philosophy on a mystical dimension of experience and an intersubjectively untestable evidence, thus reducing philosophy to a

© Springer-Verlag GmbH Germany, part of Springer Nature 2022
K. Salamun, *Karl Jaspers*, https://doi.org/10.1007/978-3-476-05896-6_12

non-objective existential philosophy and irrational metaphysics.[1] This accusation may apply to some motifs of thought in the existential philosophical period, but not to Jaspers' later thought and overall work. His versatility can be seen in the fact that he contributed original ideas, or at least ideas worthy of consideration, to many philosophical disciplines.

12.2   Philosophy of Knowledge and Science

For positivistic oriented philosophers, it may come as a surprise that Jaspers' complete works contain noteworthy contributions to the philosophy of knowledge and science. Thus, following *Kant's* epistemology, he offers differentiated reflections on the distinction between understanding and reason. He adopts Kant's term of "consciousness in general" as the central category for designating the functions of understanding in the human faculty of cognition. He emphasizes their fundamental importance for the constitution of objects (cf. W 64–70, 231–272). For the human faculty of reason, he emphasizes the importance of regulative ideas. In analogy to *Kant,* he does not ascribe to them an epistemic-constituting role, but a dynamic function activating the process of cognition. It lies in the fact that efforts to gain knowledge are never interrupted, but are always directed towards the unity, wholeness and totality of the knowledge of things, persons, facts, etc., although the goal of total knowledge is never attainable.

With the book ALLGEMEINE PSYCHOPATHOLOGIE (1913), Jaspers created one of the first scientific-theoretical works in psychiatry. The acknowledged achievement in it lies in the critique of a methodological naturalism that considers only brain-physiological and neurobiological approaches to be purposeful in explaining mental illness. In contrast, Jaspers argues for a methodological pluralism (cf. AP 1973, 20–33, 444–465, 641–651). In doing so, he by no means wants to cast doubt on the explanatory value of naturalistic theoretical approaches or even deny the principle claim to validity of the natural scientific methodological paradigm of causal explanation. Rather, he is concerned with limiting the exaggerated scope of this claim to validity in psychiatric research. He sees several mental phenomena falling through the cracks of this methodological paradigm. In order to investigate such phenomena, it is necessary to supplement the natural scientific approach with humanistic procedures of a descriptive and understanding psychology. He sees this in the phenomenological research direction of *Edmund Husserl* and in the hermeneutics of *Wilhelm Dilthey.* From *Dilthey's* remarks on the method of empathetic understanding in the humanities, Jaspers makes insights for an "*understanding* psychology" fruitful. He differentiates between several types of understanding (cf. AP 1973,

---

[1] Cf. Wolfgang Stegmüller, *Metaphysik, Skepsis, Wissenschaft,* 2. verb. Aufl. Berlin, Heidelberg, New York 1969. 214. That Stegmüller had a positive attitude towards Jaspers' existential thinking in an earlier phase of his thought was researched by Dominic Kaegi. Cf. Dominic Kaegi, Introduction by the Editor. In: ders. (Ed.), *Karl Jaspers. Schriften zur Existenzphilosophie. In: Karl Jaspers Gesamtausgabe,* vol. I/8, Basel 2018, VIII.

251–260) that are worthy of attention in psychological and psychiatric research. Among these he includes: phenomenological, static, genetic, rational, empathic, spiritual, existential, and metaphysical understanding.[2] This does not mean, however, that Jaspers was willing to accept any speculative theoretical approach that deviated from the scientific model of knowledge for psychology and psychopathology. This is clear from his strict rejection of *Sigmund Freud's* psychoanalysis (cf. AZ 59–68).[3]

In the wake of *Dilthey* and *Max Weber,* Jaspers also discusses the "Verstehen-Erklären" – dichotomy, making searching considerations about the scope of these two methods in the human sciences. He also discusses the problem of the value-free and value-bound nature of science, as well as the fundamental question of the meaning-orientation of science in general, at an appealing level (cf. MW 1958, 86–98, and KlSch 1974, 93–103).

12.3 Philosophy of Culture and History

Jaspers makes an original contribution to this with his assumption of a cultural Axial Age in human history. From the basis of his liberal conception of man, he criticizes with good arguments deterministic interpretations of history, which were represented in the philosophy of history by *Oswald Spengler, Arnold Toynbee* and *Karl Marx* (cf. UZG 13–15, 162–163). For him, history has no immanent sense running towards a final goal of the historical process. The future is "open" and depends on the unpredictable actions of human beings.

With the Axial Age thesis Jaspers is of the opinion that in the development of mankind there was a period of time (between 800 and 200 BC) in which significant cultural foundations and categories of thought were created independently of each other in China, India and the Occident. These are still effective today and still influence thinking and life in the modern age.

12.4 Philosophy of Religion and Metaphysics

In these areas, transcendence, encompassing (umgreifendes Sein), and philosophical faith are often discussed ideas. Jaspers' plea for a philosophical faith in reason as an alternative to religious faith in revelation poses a strong challenge to religious believers and theologians. To what extent Jaspers' massive criticism of denominational, religious faith viewpoints is related to a narrowed concept of religion. To

---

[2] Cf. Dietrich von Engelhardt, Zur Typologie des Verstehens bei Karl Jaspers in ihrer Bedeutung für Medizin und Psychiatrie. In: *Jb. der Österreichischen Karl-Jaspers-Gesellschaft,* Vol. 29 (2016), 11–45.

[3] Cf: Matthias Bormuth, *Lebensführung in der Moderne. Karl Jaspers und die Psychoanalyse,* Stuttgart 2002, 27–58.

what extent his criticism of the church is still applicable today cannot be answered so easily and would have to be clarified by empirical research.

12.5   Philosophical Anthropology and Ethics

Jaspers' existential philosophy is concerned with the question of the meaning of human existence. He discusses the possibility of individual self-realization in the encounter with borderline situations (death, suffering, struggle, guilt) and in interpersonal communication. From the position of a liberal ethos of humanity he is concerned with the preservation of personal freedom, individuality and the irreplaceability of each individual. The values that Jaspers associates with the ideal of interpersonal communication prove him to be an advocate of basic humanitarian values for interpersonal relationships: Truthfulness, intellectual integrity, openness, recognition of the equal status of relationship partners, willingness to take responsibility, unconditional helpfulness.

12.6   Philosophy of Education and Learning

In this field, Jaspers deals with the idea of the university, with the relationship between authority and education, as well as with the difference between traditional humanistic education and technical specified education. He argues for a personal education that is oriented toward humane values. If he published books on DIE IDEE DER UNIVERSITÄT at different periods of his thought development (1921, 1946, and 1958), this speaks for the fact that questions of education and learning were always a concern to him. In doing so, he emphasizes the value of the "scientific way of thinking" and the humane value principles associated with this way of thinking.

12.7   History of Philosophy

Jaspers intended to write a world history of philosophy. He was only able to publish the volume DIE GROSSEN PHILOSOPHEN (THE GREAT PHILOSOPHERS, 1957) before the end of his life. The extent of this project becomes clear in its entirety from the writings of his estate. The fact that the published volume deals with Asian thinkers and founders of religions, such as *Buddha, Confucius, Lao-tse* and *Nagarjuna* (cf. GP 128–185, 898–955), proves the cosmopolitanism of his humanistic thinking. With this huge project he wanted to refer to existential basic problems and fundamental questions of meaning of human existence, which he called "philosophia perennis". This "eternal philosophy" should be significant for all times of human history and in all cultures.

12.8   Political Philosophy

Jaspers' liberal ethos of humanity is the foundation of his effort to defend the pluralistic-democratic model of society of the European political tradition against all other models of society. From the liberal ethos of humanity and the "idea of democracy", authoritarian social systems and totalitarian ideologies must be consistently opposed. Through enlightenment efforts and appeals to the reason of politicians and citizens, a supra-national "community of reason-oriented individuals" should be created. This should spread a new, "moral-political way of thinking" and thus relativize the widely dominating power and interest politics. With the ideal of the reasonable, enlightened, democratically minded citizen, Jaspers closely connects the task of criticizing totalitarian ideological ways of thinking.

Impact and Topicality

13.1 Reception in Europe and Non-European Countries

Jaspers' major works have been translated into English, French, Italian, Spanish, and Japanese. Excerpts from them, as well as articles and essays, have been translated into more than 32 languages, including Arabic, Chinese, Danish, Korean, Dutch, Persian, Polish, Portuguese, Russian, Swedish, Serbo-Croatian, Turkish, and Hungarian.[1] The international reception of Jaspers' philosophy is also promoted by International Jaspers Conferences. One such conference is held continuously as part of the World Congresses of Philosophy, organized every five years by the *Fédération International des Societés de Philosophie*. The tradition of these conferences, founded by an American and a German Jaspers scholar *(Leonard H. Ehrlich* and *Richard Wisser)*, goes back to the World Congress in Montreal (1983). Usually, these conferences are hosted by the *International Association of Jaspers Societies (IAJS)*. In 2018, this conference was held as part of the 24th World Congress of Philosophy in Beijing, and this time it was organized by the *Karl Jaspers Society of North America (KJSNA)*.

In Europe, *international symposia* on Jaspers had been held every two years since 2000 until 2020 within the framework of the *Johann Wolfgang von Goethe Foundation Basel*. The venue for these autumn conferences was Klingenthal Castle (Alsace) in France. There, usually Jaspers scholars from five to seven European countries met for lectures and an exchange of ideas on new insights and interpretive hypotheses on Jaspers' multifaceted thought. The results were published in the Yearbook of the *Austrian Karl Jaspers Society*, which organized this event together with the *Karl Jaspers Foundation Basel*. Several Jaspers Societies are endeavoring to disseminate Jaspers' philosophy. In addition to societies that have existed for some time in Switzerland (Karl Jaspers Foundation Basel), Austria (Austrian Karl Jaspers Society), the USA (Karl Jaspers Society of North America) and Japan

---

[1] Cf. Christian Rabanus (ed.), *Primärbibliographie der Schriften Karl Jaspers'*, Tübingen, Basel 2000, 337–366.

© Springer-Verlag GmbH Germany, part of Springer Nature 2022
K. Salamun, *Karl Jaspers*, https://doi.org/10.1007/978-3-476-05896-6_13

(Jaspers Society of Japan), further societies have recently been founded in Poland (Krakow), Italy (Naples), Croatia (Zagreb) and Germany (Oldenburg).

It is astonishing how much attention Jaspers' thinking has received outside Europe, especially in Japan. The first beginnings of the reception of his thoughts there go back to the year 1933. From that year on, the books DIE GEISTIGE SITUATION DER ZEIT and PHILOSOPHIE were already being discussed at Japanese Universities. After the Second World War, a Jaspers Society was founded in Tokyo at the beginning of the 1950s, which published a report organ in Japanese under the title *"Existenz" (Existence)*. Later it was renamed to *"Communication"*. This continuous periodical informs about monographs written about Jaspers in Japan, as well as documenting the breadth of Jaspers' reception there. In 1970, a new foundation took place under the name *"Jaspers Society of Japan"*. It is based at Waseda University in Tokyo. Among the younger Jaspers researchers in Japan are *Yukio Masubushi, Kazuteru Fukui, Sawako Hanyu, Shinji Hayashida, Kazuko Hara, Tsuyoshi Nakayama* and *Akihiko Hirano*.

Why Jaspers' philosophy has an exceptionally strong resonance in Japan can be attributed to two reasons: The philosopher of education *Yukio Masubushi* has pointed to one of them. He argues, that Jaspers' philosophy found a special resonance after Japan's defeat in the Second World War. At the time, it was a matter of finding new humane ideals as educational counterpoints to the technological spirit of the militaristic period in Japanese history. With Jaspers, the concept of an "existential reason" was found as a point of contact. This understanding of reason does not reduce reason to mere technical rationality, but in connection with the concept of existence also pleads for an ethos of humanity and for individual-moral value attitudes. These were in particular demanded not only in post-war Japan to fill the moral-ideological vacuum of meaning. Those attitudes are also current in the present as counterpoints to an inhuman turbo-capitalism and the associated efficiency ideology.[2]

A second reason for Jaspers' reception in Japan and other Asian countries (India, South Korea, China) is the fact that Jaspers is one of the few European philosophers who has dealt with the lives and philosophical thoughts of Asian scholars and founders of religions (cf. the book DIE GROSSEN PHILOSOPHEN). This has the consequence that Asian thinkers are stimulated to reflect whether central concepts in Jaspers, such as "transcendence", "encompassing being", "borderline situation", "failing" or "foundering", "ciphers of transcendence", and "elucidation of existence", show certain similarities with Asian thoughts in religion and philosophy. Thus, attention has been drawn to similarities between *Lao-tse*'s "Tao" and Jaspers' "transcendence."[3] A Japanese philosopher pointed to parallels with *Confucius* and to similarities

---

[2] Cf. Yukio Masubushi, Zur Rezeption von Jaspers' Philosophie in Japan als Philosophie der existentiellen Vernunft. In: *Jb. der Österreichischen Karl-Jaspers-Gesellschaft*, Jg. 5 (1992), 54–56.

[3] Cf. Young do Chung, Karl Jaspers and Lao-tse. Parallels between the Concepts of Transcendence and Tao. In: *Jb. der Österreichischen Karl-Jaspers-Gesellschaft*, Jg. 11 (1998), 28–43; Young do Chung, Jaspers's Interpretation of Lao-tzu. In: Kurt Salamun, Gregory J. Walters (eds.), *Karl Jaspers's Philosophy: Expositions and Interpretations*, Amhurst 2008, 313–321.

between Jaspers' "encompassing" and the Japanese concept of "kokoro" in the sense of an all-encompassing primordial ground of all being.[4] The Japanese Jaspers scholar *Kazuteru Fukui* drew attention to the reception of the idea of encompassing being by the influential and prominent Japanese philosophers *Hajime Tanabe* and *Kitaro Nishida*.[5]

The fact that Jaspers in DIE GROSSEN PHILOSOPHEN not only treats thinkers from the Greek occidental tradition, but also pays tribute to Asian thinkers and founders of religions, such as *Buddha, Confucius, Lao-tse, Nagarjuna* (cf. GP 128–185, 898–955) in their importance for world culture, leads representatives of an intercultural philosophy to refer to him.[6] The global intercultural significance of Jaspers' understanding of philosophy is also pointed out, for example, by the Indian Jaspers scholar *Indu Sarin*, who has worked out obvious similarities between Jaspers and *Buddha*.[7]

In Italy, Jaspers was first discussed at length in 1940 by the historian of philosophy *Luigi Pareyson* (1918–1991). He wrote a monograph on Jaspers' existential philosophy. Philosophers *Enzo Paci* (1911–1976) and *Nicolo Abbagnano* (1901–1990), considered Italian existentialists, have also dealt with Jaspers' existential philosophical thought.[8] At a number of Italian universities, philosophers teach and publish on Jaspers in Italian. A broad discussion of various aspects of Jaspers' philosophy can be found in the works of *Giorgio Penzo* (1925–2006). He is considered the most prominent representative of the Catholic Jaspers reception in Italy. His main interest was Jaspers' understanding of God, the idea of transcendence, the concept of cypher, as well as the conception of philosophical faith.

The moral philosophical side of Jaspers' philosophy is the focus of *Giuseppe Cantillo*'s interest in Jaspers. At the University "Federico II" in Naples, he founded a focus for the study of Jaspers' psychological and philosophical thoughts. From there many impulses for younger Jaspers-interested scholars in Italy came forth. A *Società Italiana Karl Jaspers* was founded and two continuous publications on Jaspers research are published: *Studi Jaspersiani* and *Rivista annuale della "Società*

---

[4] Cf. Sawako Hanyu, Jaspers's Interpretation of Confucius. In: Kurt Salamun, Gregory J. Walters (eds.), *Karl Jaspers's Philosophy: Expositions and Interpretations*, Amhurst 2008, 331.

[5] Cf. Kazuteru Fukui, Zur Rezeption und Resonanz von Karl Jaspers' Philosophie in Japan. In: Reinhard Schulz, Giandomenico Bonanni et al. (eds.), *"Wahrheit ist, was uns verbindet", Karl Jaspers' Kunst zu Philosophieren*, Göttingen 2009, 340–342.

[6] Cf. Ram Adar Mall, *Philosophie im Vergleich der Kulturen. Interkulturelle Philosophie – eine neue Orientierung*, Darmstadt 1996, 159; Ram Adar Mall, Interkulturelle Philosophie und deren Ansätze bei Jaspers. In: Reiner Wiehl, Dominic Kaegi (eds.), *Karl Jaspers – Philosophie und Politik*, Heidelberg 1999, 145–162; Andreas Cesana, Karl Jaspers und die Herausforderung der interkulturellen Philosophie. In: *Jb. der Österreichischen Karl-Jaspers-Gesellschaft*, Jg. 13 (2000), 69–87.

[7] Cf. Indu Sarin, Karl Jaspers and Asian Thought. Buddha and Nagarjuna. In: Kurt Salamun, Gregory J. Walters (eds.), *Karl Jaspers's Philosophy: Expositions and Interpretations*, 291–310; Indu Sarin, *The Global Vision/Karl Jaspers*, Bern 2009, 179–204.

[8] On the Jaspers reception in Italy, see also: Stefania Achella, Karl Jaspers in Italien vor und nach 1945. In: *Offener Horizont. Jahrbuch der Karl Jaspers-Gesellschaft*, 2, 2015, ed. by Matthias Bormuth, Göttingen 2015, 58–65.

Italiana Karl Jaspers". The editors are *Cantillo* and *Francesco Miano*, who teaches in Rome, and *Stefania Achella* teaching at the University of Chieti-Pescaraand Elena Alessiato teaching in Naples.

In France, the main representatives of French Existentialism, *Sartre and Camus*, dealt with Jaspers only superficially. *Gabriel Marcel* was the one who dealt with Jaspers' thoughts most thoroughly. Among other things, he welcomed the basic communicative trait of Jaspers' philosophy and wrote an in-depth interpretation of individual borderline situations. But he also thinks that Jaspers has made an "inappropriate secularization" of concepts such as guilt, foundering and did not consider that these concepts are ultimately religious in their substance.[9]

In recent French philosophy, Jaspers' influences can be traced to *Paul Ricoeur* (1913–2005), who, among other aspects, dealt with Jaspers' understanding of God and faith.[10] Other significant philosophers from the French-speaking world who were contemporaries of Jaspers and engaged with his philosophy include: *Jean Wahl* (1888–1974), *Raymond Aron* (1905–1983), *Xaviere Tilliette,* and especially *Jeanne Hersch* (1910–2000). Hersch was a student of Jaspers in Basel. She wrote not only numerous French articles on Jaspers' ideas, but also an introduction to his philosophy, which also appeared in German translation.[11] As a professor at the University of Geneva, she founded the *"Karl Jaspers Foundation"* in Basel, already mentioned here. As its president for many years, she was concerned with financing the publication of the estate's writings. In the commemorative year of the 100th anniversary of Jaspers' birth, an issue of the *"Revue International de Philosophie"* dedicated to Jaspers was published on her initiative. Within the framework of UNESCO, both a "Table Ronde" discussion on "Karl Jaspers et l'idee d'une Philosophie universelle: ethique et avenir de l'humanité" and a Jaspers memorial exhibition were organized in Paris. A younger French Jaspers scholar, *Jean-Claude Gens,* who focuses on the connection between psychology and philosophy in Jaspers, teaches at the Departement de Philosophie at the Université de Bourgogne. He wrote a comprehensive French biography of Jaspers.[12]

In the Anglo-Saxon-speaking world, especially in the USA, Jaspers was especially honored with the volume THE PHILOSOPHY OF KARL JASPERS, published in 1957. This volume appeared in the widely known series *"Library of Living Philosophers"* edited by *Paul Arthur Schilpp*. Special credit for the dissemination of Jaspers' philosophy in the United States goes to *Edith Ehrlich,* a former listener to Jaspers in Basel, and her husband *Leonard H. Ehrlich*. Both wrote translations of Jaspers' texts into English, *Leonard Ehrlich* spread thoughts of Jaspers through his many years of teaching at the University of Massachusetts at Amherst. That Anglo-American philosophers have written a number of respectable Jaspers monographs is

---

[9] Cf. Gabriel Marcel, Grundsituation und Grenzsituation bei Karl Jaspers. In: Hans Saner (ed.), *Karl Jaspers in der Diskussion,* München 1973, 155–180.

[10] Paul Ricoeur, Philosophie und Religion bei Karl Jaspers. In: Paul A. Schilpp (ed.), *Karl Jaspers,* Stuttgart 1957, 604–635.

[11] Cf. Jeanne Hersch, *Karl Jaspers,* Lausanne 1978.

[12] Cf. Jean-Claude Gens, *Karl Jaspers. Biographie,* Paris 2003.

evidenced by books by *Charles F. Wallraff* (publication year 1970), *Oswald O. Schrag (1971)*, *Leonard H. Ehrlich (1975)*, *Alan M. Olson (1979)*, *Elisabeth Young-Bruehl* (1981), and *Gregory J. Walters (1988)*.[13] Much of the research on Jaspers is done within the framework of the *Karl Jaspers Society of North America*, founded by *Leonard Ehrlich* and *George Pepper* in 1980. This society organizes annual symposia on Jaspers at regional APA congresses (APA =American Philosophical Association). The results of these conferences are published on an ongoing basis, most recently in the form of an online journal entitled *"Existenz" (Existence)*. The popularity of Jaspers in the USA is also due to the popularity of his former student *Hannah Arendt* (1906–1975). During her lifetime, she was concerned with the translation and dissemination of Jaspers' writings in the United States. Today, when dissertations are written on her own work by American students, reference is often made to the influence Jaspers (along with Heidegger) had on her development of thought. In England, *Chris Thornhill* distinguished himself as a profound Jaspers scholar.[14]

The impact of Jaspers in the German-speaking world is difficult to assess. On the one hand, the high circulation figures of his books suggest a great impact, on the other hand, he did not leave behind a generation of students in the academic field, as *Heidegger* did. Jaspers resisted educating "disciples" out of the conviction that philosophizing could not be taught by imparting substantive knowledge. His departure for Switzerland also affected his impact on the philosophical scientific community in Germany, as did the fact that he was unable to give lectures at philosophy congresses due to his illness. *Helmut Fahrenbach* has shown that Jaspers must have had a decisive influence on one of the internationally best-known contemporary German philosophers, *Jürgen Habermas*. The concept of "communicative reason" used by *Habermas* has obvious structural similarities with Jaspers' understanding of communication and reason. *Habermas* engaged with Jaspers' thought in various contexts, as evidenced by an early engagement with Jaspers in the article "Die Gestalten der Wahrheit" (1958). He later included this article in his volume PHILOSOPHICAL-POLITICAL PROFILES as a reprint.[15] It is not uninteresting that *Habermas* referred back to Jaspers' title of the "spiritual situation of time" when he published volume 1000 of the well-known series *edition suhrkamp* in 1979. He chose for this writing the title: STICHWORTE ZUR "GEISTIGEN SITUATION DER ZEIT". In it, "time-diagnostic reviews" were published by intellectual authors with a rather left-wing orientation.

---

[13] Cf. Charles F. Wallraff, *Karl Jaspers. An Introduction to His Philosophy*, Princeton 1970; Oswald O. Schrag, *Existence, Existenz, and Transcendence. An Introduction to the Philosophy of Karl Jaspers*, Pittsburgh 1971; Leonhard H. Ehrlich, Karl Jaspers: *Philosophy as Faith*, Amherst 1975; Alan M. Olson, *Transcendence and Hermeneutics: An Interpretation of the Philosophy of Karl Jaspers*, Boston 1979; Elisabeth Young-Bruehl, *Freedom and Karl Jaspers' Philosophy*, New Haven 1981; Gregory J. Walters, *Karl Jaspers and the Role of "Conversion" in the Nuclear Age*, Lanham 1987.

[14] Cf. Chris Thornhill, *Karl Jaspers. Politics and metaphysics*, London, New York 2002.

[15] Cf. Jürgen Habermas, *Philosophisch-politische Profile*, Frankfurt 3rd.ed. 1981, 79–109.

In the former *GDR* there was *Hans-Martin Gerlach* (1940–2011), one of the few philosophers who dealt with Jaspers from an ideologically only moderately distorted perspective. *Gerlach* appreciated the usefulness of the borderline situation conception for a medical ethics and traced the Weberian influence on Jaspers.[16]

It should not go unmentioned that in Jaspers' native town of Oldenburg, the *"Karl Jaspers Lectures on Contemporary Issues"* have been held annually at the university there since 1990, and that there is a separate Karl Jaspers House, where Jaspers' complete working library is available for research purposes.

13.2 Precursor of Intercultural Philosophy

If Jaspers is regarded as a precursor or representative of intercultural philosophy, this is the consequence of his thoughts on the philosophia perennis, his project of the world history of philosophy, as well as the thesis of an Axial Age in history. By philosophia perennis, Jaspers understands an open, intellectual reservoir of reflections on the eternal fundamental questions of the conditio humana. Philosophers from all cultures of the world can contribute to it. However, the philosophia perennis can never become the property of just one cultural or national group of philosophers.[17]

As the project of the World History of Philosophy proves, Jaspers was a multicultural thinking philosopher. In his World History, outstanding thinkers and creative people – philosophers, founders of religions, artists – from different cultures must be appreciated. The fact that in DIE GROSSEN PHILOSOPHEN he discusses thoughts of Chinese and Indian founders of religions and worldviews and recognize them as contributions to world culture is a proof of his counter-position to the Eurocentric viewpoints of *Hegel and Heidegger*. The latter saw the origin of philosophy merely in ancient Greece and thus in Europe.

In the interculturality-debate, the Axial Age thesis is appreciated as an important philosophical basis for intercultural efforts of mutual understanding different cultures. Jaspers is regarded as a pioneer of an open, unrestricted understanding of philosophy because of his referring to the threefold origin of philosophy in China, India and the Occident. With his philosophy of the "open horizon" he created a platform for dialogue between culturally different understandings of philosophy.[18]

---

[16] Cf. Hans-Martin Gerlach, *Existenzphilosophie und Politik. Kritische Auseinandersetzung mit Karl Jaspers,* Berlin (DDR) 1974, 78–92.

[17] Cf. Ram Adar Mall, *Philosophie im Vergleich der Kulturen. Interkulturelle Philosophie – eine neue Orientierung,* Darmstadt 1996, 159.

[18] Cf. Andreas Cesana, Karl Jaspers und die Herausforderung der interkulturellen Philosophie. In: *Jb. der Österreichischen Karl-Jaspers-Gesellschaft,* 13 (2000), 86.

13.3   The Axial Age Thesis as an Impulse for Research in Religious, Social and Cultural Studies

Since the eighties of the last century, the Axial Age thesis has experienced an aston-ishing renaissance. It is increasingly discussed in the context of studies in the fields of sociology of religion, comparative cultural and civilization theory, as well as the theory of modernity and globalization. The renaissance is particularly evident in English-language publications, which, with reference to Jaspers, speak of an "Axial period", an "Axial stage in world history", "Axial civilizations", "Axial transforma-tions", "Axial breakthrough", "Axial turns", an "Axial moment" in world history or an "Axial model".

The Israeli sociologist and religious scholar *Shmuel N. Eisenstadt* (1923–2010) deserves a great deal of credit for disseminating Jaspers' Axial Age thesis.[19] He played a leading role in planning and organizing conferences and research programs that addressed the following questions: What were the social and political precondi-tions for the cultural revolutions and intellectual awakenings claimed in Jaspers' Axial Age thesis for China, India, and the Occident? Are there common structural features that were responsible for the cultural upheavals occurring in the three inde-pendent regions? Was it the breaking apart of rigid mythical-monistic conceptions of world order and the emergence of new, dualistic interpretations of the world (for *Eisenstadt*: "transcendental visions")? Did this open up the possibility of opposing the earthly order with a supra-earthly order and, from this, questioning the earthly order? Were the traditional world explanations and collective, cultural concepts of meaning shaken by new spiritual elites (prophets, philosophers, sages)? Were these able to compete with older elites, who had hitherto been considered specialists in the magical, ritual and sacred, by designing new, more individualistic and worldly-oriented concepts of meaning? Are there structural parallels between the conditions of emergence of the Axial Age cultures and the two religions of Christianity and Islam that later entered world history, as well as the scientific-technical civilization of modernity? Can the strategies for the production of collective identities and for the justification of political power in the respective cultures be compared with each other? Doesn't the Axial Age, due to the separation of spiritual and social power that occurred in it, also lie at the root of the ideological justification of earthly power and thus also of the ideologization of politics? What does human beings living in the present, owe to this early age in human development? Is the model of "Axiality" that Jaspers sketched for the period between 800 and 200 BC also transferable to later periods in history?

In such questions in comparative cultural theory, civilization theory and histori-cal sociology, Jaspers' Axial Age thesis was an important starting point. This is confirmed in a standard work on the Axial Age problem edited by the American sociologist of religion *Robert N. Bellah* (1927–2013) and the German social

---

[19] Cf. Shmuel N. Eisenstadt, *The origins and diversity of axial age civilisations*, Albany 1986; Shmuel N. Eisenstadt, *Axial civilisations and world history*, Leiden 2005; Shmuel N. Eisenstadt, *Kulturen der Achsenzeit: ihre Ursprünge und ihre Vielfalt*, Frankfurt 1967.

philosopher *Hans Joas*.[20] The Heidelberg cultural scientist and Egyptologist *Jan Assmann* has made an interesting proposal for the methodological interpretation of the Axial Age thesis, in that he does not want to understand the concept of the Axial Age as a concept of an epoch. On the basis of the criteria that Jaspers emphasized for the Axial Period upheaval, the thesis could also be understood as a "cultural-analytical heuristic".

> As a cultural-analytical probe, however, the Axial Age Theorem is an excellent instrument that has accompanied and infinitely promoted my own Egyptological work, for example. If I have succeeded to some extent in turning Egyptology into a cultural science, then it is thanks to the Jaspersian probe, which guided me from the very beginning not to lose sight of the cultural-philosophical perspective above all the philological and archaeological detail work.[21]

By the way, *Assmann* also gave a knowledgeable account of the emergence of the discussion about an Axial Age in world history from the French Orientalist *Abraham Anquetil-Dupperon* to the present day in *Shmuel N. Eisenstadt* and *Robert N. Bellah*.[22]

13.4   Effect on German Policy?

As far as Jaspers' impact on political events in the FRG (Federal Republic of Germany) is concerned, at least two points could be emphasized. One of them results from the massive criticism of the "party state" in the FRG and the tendencies towards a party oligarchy diagnosed by Jaspers. He repeatedly pleaded for a spontaneous formation of will among the people that was not bound to parties, thus preformulating many grassroots democratic arguments that have been advocated in the Federal Republic by the extra-parliamentary opposition of the New Left.

Although Jaspers did not exert any direct influence on the New Left, his publicly expressed displeasure with the established party landscape at least prepared an intellectual sounding board for left-wing criticism.

Obvious parallels can also be seen between the "Zeitgeist"- critique in DIE GEIS-TIGE SITUATION DER ZEIT and the cultural and social critique of the intellectual fathers of the New Left, *Herbert Marcuse and Max Horkheimer*. What is described by the latter as phenomena of "alienation", "reification", "technological rationality", "one-dimensionality" of the human being in advanced industrial society, Jaspers already criticized in his early writing under the influence of *Weber's* critique

---

[20] Hans Joas, Robert N. Bellah (eds.), *The Axial Age and its Consequences for Subsequent History and the Present,* Cambridge MA. 2012; see also: Hans Joas, *Was ist die Achsenzeit? Eine wissenschaftliche Debatte als Diskurs über Transzendenz,* Basel 2014.

[21] Jan Assmann, Karl Jaspers' Theory of Axis Age as a Cultural Analytical Heuristic. In: *Offener Horizont. Jahrbuch der Karl Jaspers-Gesellschaft,* 4/2017, ed. by Matthias Bormuth, Göttingen 2017, 53.

[22] Jan Assmann, *Achsenzeit – Eine Archäologie der Moderne,* München 2018.

of rationalization as tendencies of "rationalization, mathematization and mechanization of the world" (GSZ 21) that are hostile to individuality. Jaspers also already anticipated the critique of the anonymizing and leveling tendencies of individuals, which for the representatives of Critical Theory are typical of modern industrial societies.

From today's perspective, it can be said that Jaspers, with his publicly expressed thesis about a necessary reversal in the West-German "Ostpolitik" against the communist state of Eastern Germany, gave impulses for a dialogue between the formerer two separated parts of Germany. The German Foreign Ministry was involved in the preparation of the change of course in West German foreign policy. This change of course was later brought about by the social-liberal coalition *(Brandt/Scheel)* and was no longer a controversial point of conflict between the two major parties of the time, the CDU and the SPD, until German reunification in 1990.

Jaspers' recommendations for the foreign policy of the Federal Republic of Germany at that time with regard to the connection to the West in a European confederation and the behavior of the FRG towards the second German state, the GDR, were later appreciated by the former Federal Chancellor *Willy Brandt*. He wrote a foreword to the new edition of Jaspers' book FREIHEIT UND WIEDERVEREINIGUNG (1990). In it he distanced himself from some points of criticism ('Jaspers'criticism of the Federal German Law, his criticism of the idea of the nation state), but Brandt confirmed Jaspers in many of his speculative political arguments.

> Incidentally, some of us who helped a new policy achieve a breakthrough at the end of the sixties, beginning of the seventies – against much ignorance and impertinence – were aware of the proximity to essential Jaspersian postulates: The primacy of freedom was undisputed for us, as was the clear yes to European unification and, under the given world-political conditions, to the Western alliance … with Jaspers there was the conviction that technical arrangements with those responsible for the other part of Germany were legitimate and that, especially in the face of difficult partners, the attempt at conversation had to be undertaken again and again. In his words: Talking to each other – especially with the communists, the Russians – was the great task. Moreover, he did not give up hope that in a new world situation the leadership of the Soviet Union would one day change its will. Yes, he already reckoned that Russia might "slowly turn in on itself." (FW 1990, II-III)

During his tenure as Federal Minister of Foreign Affairs, *Brandt* expressed his appreciation for Jaspers in the following congratulatory telegram dated 22nd February 1968:

> On the occasion of your 85th birthday today, may I offer you my warmest congratulations and best wishes for your personal well-being. You have not only made yourself heard worldwide with your philosophical life's work, but have also made a strong impact with your critical contributions to politics. Your resistance to tyranny and uniformity has set an example to many.

References

Achella, Stefania: Europa – wohin soll es gehen? Jaspers bei den Rencontres internationales de Genève (1946). In: *Jahrbuch der Österreichischen Karl-Jaspers-Gesellschaft*, 26 (2013), 87–116.

Achella, Stefania: Karl Jaspers in Italien vor und nach 1945. In: *Offener Horizont. Jahrbuch der Karl Jaspers-Gesellschaft,*2/2015, hg. von Matthias Bormuth, Göttingen 2015, 58–65.

Arendt, Hannah: Karl Jaspers. Wahrheit, Freiheit und Friede. Reden zur Verleihung des Friedenspreises des Deutschen Buchhandels 1958, München 1958.

Arendt, Hannah: Vita activa oder vom tätigen Leben, München1996a.

Arendt, Hannah/Blücher, Heinrich: *Briefe 1936–1968,* hg. mit einer Einführung von Lotte Köhler, München 1996b.

Aron, Raymond: Karl Jaspers und die Politik. In: Jeanne Hersch, u. a. (Hg.): *Karl Jaspers. Philosoph – Arzt – politischer Denker.*Symposium zum 100. Geburtstag in Basel und Heidelberg, München 1986, 59–76.

Assmann, Aleida: Jaspers' Achsenzeit, oder: Vom Glück und Elend der Zentralperspektive in der Geschichte. In: Dietrich Harth (Hg.): *Karl Jaspers. Denken zwischen Wissenschaft, Politik und Philosophie*, Stuttgart 1989, 187–205.

Assmann, Jan: Karl Jaspers' Theorie der Achsenzeit als kulturanalytische Heuristik. In: *Offener Horizont. Jahrbuch der Karl Jaspers-Gesellschaft*, 4/2017, hg. von Matthias Bormuth, Göttingen 2017, 43–55.

Assmann, Jan: *Achsenzeit – Eine Archäologie der Moderne*, München 2018.

Barth, Karl: *Die kirchliche Dogmatik*, 3. Bd., 2. Teil, Zürich 1948.

Baumgartner, Eduard: Zur Erinnerung an die Jaspers'sche Form, Streitgespräche – feindlich und freundlich – fort und fort in Gang zu halten. In: Klaus Piper, Hans Saner (Hg.): *Erinnerungen an Karl Jaspers*, München, Zürich 1974, 123–146.

Becker, Werner: Der fernethische Illusionismus und die Realität. In: Kurt Salamun (Hg.): *Aufklärungsperspektiven. Weltanschauungsanalyse und Ideologiekritik*, Tübingen 1989, 1–8.

Bellah Robert N./Joas, Hans (eds.): *The Axial Age and its Consequences,* Cambridge MA 2012.

Bernstein, Adolf: Erinnerungen an Karl Jaspers. In: Klaus Piper, Hans Saner (Hg.): *Erinnerungen an Karl Jaspers*, München, Zürich 1974, 289–295.

Beyme Klaus von: Karl Jaspers – Vom philosophischen Außenseiter zum *Praeceptor Germaniae*. In: *Heidelberg 1945,*hg. von Jürgen C. Heß, Hartmut Lehmann und Volker Sellin in Verbindung mit Detlev Junker und Eike Wolgast, Stuttgart 1996, 130–148.

Bollnow, Otto Friedrich: Existenzerhellung und philosophische Anthropologie. Versuch einer Auseinandersetzung mit Karl Jaspers. In: Hans Saner (Hg.): *Karl Jaspers in der Diskussion*, München 1973a, 185–223.

Bollnow, Otto Friedrich: *Existenzphilosophie und Geschichte. Versuch einer Auseinandersetzung mit Karl Jaspers*. In: Hans Saner (Hg.): *Karl Jaspers in der Diskussion*, München 1973b, 235–273.

Bonanni, Giandomenico: Die Katholizität und ihre Methoden. In: Anton Hügli, Dominic Kaegi, Bernd Weidmann (Hg.):*Existenz und Sinn. Karl Jaspers im Kontext,*Heidelberg 2009, 159–186.

Bormuth, Matthias: Lebensführung in der Moderne. Karl Jaspers und die Psychoanalyse, Stuttgart 2002.

Burkard, Franz P.:*Ethische Existenz bei Karl Jaspers*, Würzburg 1982.

Burkard, Franz P.: Existenzphilosophie und Strebensethik. In:*Jahrbuch der Österreichischen Karl-Jaspers-Gesellschaft*, Bd. 12 (1999), 29–41.

Camus, Albert: *Der Mensch in der Revolte*, aus dem Französischen übertragen von Justus Streller, Reinbek 1980.

Cesana, Andreas: Karl Jaspers und die Herausforderung der interkulturellen Philosophie. In: *Jb. der Österreichischen Karl-Jaspers-Gesellschaft*, Bd. 13 (2000), 69–87.

Cesana, Andreas: Karl Jaspers' Idee der Weltphilosophie und das Problem der Einheit des Denkens. In: Reinhard Schulz, Giandomenico Bonanni, Matthias Bormuth (Hg.):*„ Wahrheit ist, was uns verbindet", Karl Jaspers' Kunst zu Philosophieren*, Göttingen 2009, 315–328.

De Rosa, Renato: Politische Akzente im Leben eines Philosophen. Karl Jaspers in Heidelberg 1901–1946. In: Nachwort zu: ders. (Hg.): *Karl Jaspers, Erneuerung der Universität. Reden und Schriften 1945/46*, Heidelberg 1986.

Drescher, Wilhelmine: *Erinnerungen an Karl Jaspers in Heidelberg*, Meisenheim am Glan 1975.

Dufour, Gabrielle und Alfred: *Schwierige Freiheit. Gespräche mit Jeanne Hersch*, München, Zürich 1990.

Dutt, Carsten/Wolgast, Eike (Hg.): *Karl Jaspers Korrespondenzen: Politik – Universität*, Göttingen 2016.

Earle, William A.: Die Anthropologie in Jaspers' Philosophie. In: Paul A. Schilpp (Hg.): *Karl Jaspers*, Stuttgart 1957, 515–531.

Ehrlich, Leonard H.: Tolerance and the Prospect of a World Philosophy. In: Leonard H. Ehrlich, Richard Wisser (eds.): *Karl Jaspers Today. Philosophy at the Threshold of the Future*, Washington D. C. 1988, 93–100.

Eisenstadt, Shmuel N.: *The origins and diversity of axial age civilisations*, Albany 1986.

Eisenstadt, Shmuel N. (Hg.): *Kulturen der Achsenzeit: Ihre Ursprünge und ihre Vielfalt*. Teil I: Griechenland, Israel, Mesopotamien, und Teil II: Spätantike, Indien, China, Islam, Frankfurt 1987.

Eisenstadt, Shmuel N. u. a. (eds.): *Axial civilisations and world history*, Leiden 2005.

Engelhardt, Dietrich von: Zur Typologie des Verstehens bei Karl Jaspers in ihrer Bedeutung für Medizin und Psychiatrie. In: *Jb. der Österreichischen Karl-Jaspers-Gesellschaft*, Bd. 29 (2016), 11–45.

Fahrenbach, Helmut: Kommunikative Vernunft – ein zentraler Bezugspunkt zwischen Karl Jaspers und Jürgen Habermas. In: Kurt Salamun (Hg.): *Karl Jaspers – Zur Aktualität seines Denkens*, München 1991, 189–216.

Fahrenbach, Helmut: Existenzdialektische Ethik. In: Annemarie Pieper (Hg.): *Geschichte der neueren Ethik*, Bd. 1, Tübingen, Basel 1992, 256–283.

Farias, Victor: *Heidegger und der Nationalsozialismus*, Frankfurt 1989.

Fonfara, Dirk: Einleitung des Herausgebers. In: ders. (Hg.): Ausgewählte Verlags- und Übersetzerkorrespondenzen. In: *Karl Jaspers Gesamtausgabe*, Bd. III/8.1, Basel 2018, XXIX–XCV.

Fukui, Kazuteru: Zur Rezeption und Resonanz von Karl Jaspers' Philosophie in Japan. In: Reinhard Schulz, Giandomenico Bonanni, Matthias Bormuth (Hg.): *„ Wahrheit ist, was uns verbindet", Karl Jaspers' Kunst zu Philosophieren*, Göttingen 2009, 338–348.

Gadamer, Hans Georg: Philosophische Begegnungen. In: ders.: *Hermeneutik im Rückblick, Gesammelte Werke, 10. Bd.*, Tübingen 1995.

Geiger, Theodor: *Die Masse und ihre Aktion. Ein Beitrag zur Soziologie der Revolutionen.*Stuttgart 1926.

Gens, Jean-Claude: Karl Jaspers Biographie, Paris 2003.

Gens, Jean-Claude: Zur Jaspers-Rezeption in der französischen Philosophie und Psychiatrie. In: *Jb. der Österreichischen Karl-Jaspers-Gesellschaft*, 26 (2013), 65–86.

Gerhard, Volker: Existentieller Liberalismus. Zur Konzeption der Politik bei Karl Jaspers. In: Reiner Wiehl, Dominic Kaegi (Hg.): *Karl Jaspers – Philosophie und Politik*, Heidelberg 1999, 97–114.

Gerlach, Hans-Martin: *Existenzphilosophie und Politik. Kritische Auseinandersetzung mit Karl Jaspers*, Berlin (DDR) 1974.

Habermas, Jürgen: Philosophisch-politische Profile, 1981, 79–109.

Habermas, Jürgen (Hg.): *Stichworte zur „Geistigen Situation der Zeit". Bd. 1: Nation und Republik*, Einleitung, Frankfurt am Main 1979.

Hanyu, Sawako: Jaspers's Interpretation of Konfuzius. In: Kurt Salamun, Gregory J. Walters (eds.): *Karl Jaspers's Philosophy. Expositions and Interpretations*, Amherst 2008, 321–335.

Harth, Dietrich (Hg.): *Karl Jaspers. Denken zwischen Wissenschaft, Politik und Philosophie*, Stuttgart 1989.

Hayek, Friedrich von: *Der Weg zur Knechtschaft*, Erlenbach-Zürich o. J.

Heidegger Martin/Jaspers Karl: *Briefwechsel 1920–1963*, hg. von Walter Biemel und Hans Saner, Frankfurt, München, Zürich 1990.

Henrich, Dieter: Denken im Blick auf Max Weber. In: *Karl Jaspers: Max Weber. Gesammelte Schriften*, Mit einer Einführung von Dieter Henrich, München, Zürich 1988, 7–31.

Hersch, Jeanne: Karl Jaspers als Lehrer. In: *Offener Horizont. Festschrift für Karl Jaspers*, hg. von Klaus Piper, München 1953, 440–442.

Hersch, Jeanne: *Karl Jaspers. Eine Einführung in sein Werk*, München 1980.

Hersch, Jeanne u. a. (Hg.): *Karl Jaspers. Philosoph – Arzt – politischer Denker*, Symposium zum 100. Geburtstag in Basel und Heidelberg, München 1986.

Hochhuth, Rolf: Lebensfreundlichkeit. In: Klaus Piper, Hans Saner (Hg.), *Erinnerungen an Karl Jaspers*, München, Zürich 1974, 297–303.

Höffe, Otfried: Tugend. In: ders.: *Lexikon der Ethik*, 6. Neubearb. Aufl. München 2002, 267–270.

Horn, Hermann (Hg.): *Karl Jaspers: Was ist Erziehung? Ein Lesebuch*, Textauswahl und Zusammenstellung von Hermann Horn, München 1977, 2. Aufl. 1992.

Hügli, Anton: World Philosophy: On Philosophers making Peace. In: Helmut Wautischer, Alan M. Olson, Gregory J. Walters (eds.): *Philosophical Faith and the Future of Humanity*, Heidelberg, London, New York 2012, 335–345.

Hügli, Anton: Jaspers' Darstellung der Philosophie – eine Form der indirekten Mitteilung? In: *Jb. der Österreichischen Karl-Jaspers-Gesellschaft*, Jg. 28 (2015), 9–36.

Hügli, Anton: Indirekte Mitteilung. Inwiefern es Grenzen der Mitteilung gibt. In: ders.: *Von der Schwierigkeit, vernünftig zu sein*, Basel 2016, 175–194.

Humboldt, Wilhelm von: *Werke IV.: Schriften zur Politik und zum Bildungswesen*, Stuttgart 1964.

Immel, Oliver: Einleitung des Herausgebers. In: ders. (Hg.): Karl Jaspers – Schriften zur Universitätsidee. In: *Karl Jaspers Gesamtausgabe*, Bd. I/21, Basel 2016, IV–LIX.

Immel, Oliver/Stelzer, Harald (Hg.): *Welt und Philosophie. Politik-, kultur- und sozialphilosophische Beiträge zum Denken von Karl Jaspers*, Innsbruck 2011.

Jaspers, Karl: Wahrheit und Wissenschaft. In: ders.: *Philosophische Aufsätze*, Frankfurt 1967, 62–77.

Jaspers, Karl: Wie Erinnerung an das Erlebte zur Auffassung der Gegenwart führt. Ein Gespräch über Deutschland mit Klaus Harpprecht (1962). In: Karl Jaspers: *Provokationen. Gespräche und Interviews*, hg. von Hans Saner, München 1969, 147–168.

Jaspers, Karl: *Erneuerung der Universität. Reden und Schriften 1945/46*, mit einem Nachwort hg. von Renato de Rosa, Heidelberg 1986.

Jaspers, Karl: *Max Weber. Gesammelte Schriften*. Mit einer Einführung von Dieter Henrich, München, Zürich 1988.

Jaspers, Karl: Studium 1901–1907. Teil 1. (Autobiographische Schrift, Erstveröffentlichung aus dem Nachlass, bearbeitet von Hans Saner). In: *Jb. der Österreichischen Karl-Jaspers-Gesellschaft*, Bd. 9 (1996), 9–46.

Jaspers, Karl: Studium 1901–1907. Teil 2. (Autobiographische Schrift, Erstveröffentlichung aus dem Nachlass, bearbeitet von Hans Saner). In: *Jb. der Österreichischen Karl-Jaspers-Gesellschaft*, Bd. 10 (1997), 7–54.

Jaspers, Karl/Bauer, Karl Heinrich: *Briefwechsel 1945–1968*, hg. und erläutert von Renato de Rosa, Heidelberg, New York 1983.

Jaspers, Karl/Beutler Ernst: Briefwechsel 1937–1960. In: *Karl Jaspers Korrespondenzen Bd. 2 Philosophie*, hg. von Dominic Kaegi und Reiner Wiehl, Göttingen 2013, Brief Nr. 47, S. 95.

Jaspers, Karl/Bultmann, Rudolf: *Die Frage der Entmythologisierung*, München 1981.

Jaspers, Karl/Zahrnt, Heinz: *Philosophie und Offenbarungsglaube. Ein Zwiegespräch*, Hamburg 1963.

Jaspers, Karl/Zimmer, Heinrich: *Briefe 1929–1939*, aus dem Nachlass zusammengestellt von Hans Saner und Maya Rauch. Erstmals publiziert in: *Jb. der Österreichischen Karl-Jaspers-Gesellschaft*, Jg. 6 (1993), 7–32.

Joas, Hans: *Was ist die Achsenzeit? Eine wissenschaftliche Debatte als Diskurs über Transzendenz*, Basel 2014.

Jünger, Friedrich Georg: *Die Perfektion der Technik*, Frankfurt 1946.

Kadereit, Ralf: *Karl Jaspers und die Bundesrepublik Deutschland. Politische Gedanken eines Philosophen*, Paderborn, München 1999.

Kaegi, Dominic: Was ist metaphysische Schuld? In: *Jb. der Österreichischen Karl-Jaspers-Gesellschaft*, Jg. 14 (2001), 9–39.

Kaegi, Dominic: Einleitung des Herausgebers. In: ders. (Hg.): Karl Jaspers: Schriften zur Existenzphilosophie. In: *Karl Jaspers Gesamtausgabe*, Bd. I/8, Basel 2018, VII–XLVIII.

Kant, Immanuel: Zum ewigen Frieden. In: ders.: *Werke in zehn Bänden*, Hg. von Wilhelm Weischedel, Bd. 9, 1.Teil. Darmstadt 1983a.

Kant, Immanuel: Der Streit der Fakultäten. In: ders.: *Werke in zehn Bänden*, Hg. von Wilhelm Weischedel, Bd. 9, 1.Teil. Darmstadt 1983b.

Kierkegaard, Sören: Abschließende unwissenschaftliche Nachschrift zu den Philosophischen Brocken, 1. Teil. In: ders.: *Gesammelte Werke. 16. Abt.*, Düsseldorf, Köln 1958.

Kirkbright, Suzanne: *Karl Jaspers. A Biography. Navigation in Truth*, New Haven, London 2005.

Kirkbright, Suzanne (Hg.): *Karl Jaspers Italienbriefe 1902*, Heidelberg 2006.

Knauss, Gerhard: Der Begriff des Umgreifenden in Jaspers' Philosophie. In: Paul A. Schilpp (Hg.): *Karl Jaspers*, Stuttgart 1957, 130–163.

Knauss, Gerhard: Erinnerungen an Karl Jaspers. In: Klaus Piper, Hans Saner (Hg.): *Erinnerungen an Karl Jaspers*, München, Zürich 1974, 165–172.

Koch, Hans-Albrecht: *Die Universität. Geschichte einer europäischen Institution*, Darmstadt 2008.

Koselleck, Reinhard: Jaspers, die Geschichte und das Überpolitische. In: Jeanne Hersch u. a. (Hg.): *Karl Jaspers Philosoph, Arzt, politischer Denker*, München, Zürich 1986, 291–302.

Kymlicka, Will: *Politische Philosophie heute. Eine Einführung*, Frankfurt, New York 1997.

Landmann, Michael: Erinnerung an Karl Jaspers. In: Klaus Piper, Hans Saner (Hg.): *Erinnerungen an Karl Jaspers*, München, Zürich 1974, 195–205.

Latzel, Edwin: Die Erhellung der Grenzsituationen. In: Paul A. Schilpp (Hg.), *Karl Jaspers*, Stuttgart 1957, 164–192.

Liepmann, Heinrich: Erinnerungen an Karl Jaspers aus den Jahren 1925–1936. In: Klaus Piper, Hans Saner (Hg.):*Erinnerungen an Karl Jaspers*, München, Zürich 1974, 47–52.

Lippmann, Walter: *Die Gesellschaft freier Menschen*, Bern 1945.

Löwenstein, Julius I.: Erinnerungen an Jaspers. In: Klaus Piper, Hans Saner (Hg.): *Erinnerungen an Karl Jaspers*, München, Zürich 1974, 43–45.

Löwith, Karl: *Mein Leben in Deutschland vor und nach 1933. Ein Bericht*, Stuttgart 1986.

Lübbe, Hermann: Die Masse, der Nationalsozialismus und die Atombombe, Karl Jaspers als politischer Moralist. In: Reinhard Schulz, Giandomenico Bonanni, Matthias Bormuth (Hg.), „*Wahrheit ist, was uns verbindet"Karl Jaspers' Kunst zu Philosophieren*, Göttingen 2009, 391–410.

Mall, Ram Adar: *Philosophie im Vergleich der Kulturen. Interkulturelle Philosophie – eine neue Orientierung*, Darmstadt 1996.

Mall, Ram Adar: Interkulturelle Philosophie und deren Ansätze bei Jaspers. In: Reiner Wiehl, Dominic Kaegi (Hg.): *Karl Jaspers – Philosophie und Politik*, Heidelberg 1999, 145–162.

Mann, Golo: *Erinnerungen und Gedanken. Eine Jugend in Deutschland*, Frankfurt a. M. 1986.

Marcel, Gabriel: Situation fondamentale et situations limites chez Karl Jaspers. In: *Recherches philosophique* (1932/33), dt. Grundsituation und Grenzsituation bei Karl Jaspers. In: Hans Saner (Hg.): *Karl Jaspers in der Diskussion,* München 1973, 155–180.

Masubushi, Yukio: Zur Rezeption von Jaspers' Philosophie in Japan als Philosophie der existentiellen Vernunft. In: *Jb. der Österreichischen Karl-Jaspers-Gesellschaft,* Jg. 5 (1992), 48–62.

Mayer, Ernst: *Dialektik des Nichtwissens,* Basel 1950.

Michels, Robert: *Zur Soziologie des Parteiwesens in der modernen Demokratie. Untersuchungen über die oligarchischen Tendenzen des Gruppenlebens,* Leipzig 1911.

Mitscherlich, Alexander/Weber, Alfred: *Freier Sozialismus,* Heidelberg 1946.

Nakayama, Tsuyoshi: Die Wende des ethischen Denkmotivs bei Karl Jaspers von der „Ethik der Existenz" zur „Ethik der Vernunft". In: *Jb. der Österreichischen Karl-Jaspers-Gesellschaft,* Bd. 28 (2015), 63–78.

Nietzsche, Friedrich: Götzendämmerung. In: ders.: *Sämtliche Werke. Kritische Studienausgabe in 15 Einzelbänden,* hg. von Giorgio Colli und Mazzino Montinari, Bd. 6, München 1988.

Olson, Alan M.: Metaphysical Guilt. In: *Jb. der Österreichischen Karl-Jaspers-Gesellschaft,* Bd. 26 (2013), 167–190.

Ortega y Gasset: *Der Aufstand der Massen.* Madrid 1930.

Ott, Hugo: *Martin Heidegger: unterwegs zu seiner Biographie,* Frankfurt, New York 1988.

Oyen, Hendrik van: Der philosophische Glaube. In: *Theologische Zeitschrift,* 14 (1958).

Peach, Filiz: *Death, ‚Deathlessness' and Existenz in Karl Jaspers' Philosophy,* Edinburgh 2008.

Penzo, Giorgio: Der „existentielle Jesus" bei Karl Jaspers. In: Richard Wisser, Leonard Ehrlich (Hg.): *Karl Jaspers. Philosoph unter Philosophen,* Würzburg, Amsterdam 1993, 255–271.

Pepper, George B.: Die Relevanz von Jaspers' Achsenzeit für interkulturelle Studien. In: Kurt Salamun (Hg.): *Karl Jaspers. Zur Aktualität seines Denkens,* München 1991, 70–85.

Piper, Klaus: Karl Jaspers. Erfahrungen aus verlegerischer Zusammenarbeit. In: Klaus Piper, Hans Saner (Hg.): *Erinnerungen an Karl Jaspers,* München, Zürich 1974, 185–194.

Rabanus, Christian (Hg.): *Primärbibliographie der Schriften Karl Jaspers',* Tübingen, Basel 2000.

Ricoeur, Paul: Philosophie und Religion bei Karl Jaspers. In: Paul A. Schilpp (Hg.), *Karl Jaspers,* Stuttgart 1957, 604–635.

Saage, Richard: *Politische Utopien der Neuzeit,* Darmstadt 1991.

Salamun, Kurt: *Karl Jaspers,* 2. erw. Aufl., Würzburg 2006.

Salamun, Kurt: Einleitung des Herausgebers. In: ders. (Hg.): *Karl Jaspers: Vom Ursprung und Ziel der Geschichte.* In: *Karl Jaspers Gesamtausgabe,* Bd. I/10, Basel 2017, VII–XXII.

Salamun, Kurt (Hg.): *Karl Jaspers. Zur Aktualität seines Denkens,* München, Zürich 1991.

Salamun, Kurt (Hg.): *Philosophie – Erziehung – Universität. Zu Karl Jaspers' Bildungs- und Erziehungsphilosophie,* Frankfurt 1995.

Salamun, Kurt/Walters, Gregory J. (eds.): *Karl Jaspers's Philosophy: Expositions and Interpretations,* Amherst, New York 2008.

Salamun, Kurt: Karl Jaspers: Existenzverwirklichung in der Kommunikation. In: Josef Speck (Hg.): *Grundprobleme der großen Philosophen: Philosophie der Gegenwart V,* Göttingen 1982, 9–48.

Salin, Edgar: Freundschaftliche Erinnerungen an Karl Jaspers. In: *Erinnerungen an Karl Jaspers,* hg. von Klaus Piper und Hans Saner, München, Zürich 1974, 13–23.

Saner, Hans: Vorwort zu: Karl Jaspers: *Schicksal und Wille,* hg. von Hans Saner, München 1967.

Saner, Hans: Jaspers' Idee einer kommenden Weltphilosophie. In: Leonard H. Ehrlich, Richard Wisser (eds.): *Karl Jaspers Today. Philosophy at the Threshold of the Future,* Lanham, MD 1988. 75–92.

Saner, Hans: Jaspers' Thesen zu Fragen der Hochschulerneuerung (1933) im Vergleich mit Heideggers Rektoratsrede. In: Kurt Salamun (Hg.): *Karl Jaspers. Zur Aktualität seines Denkens,* München 1991, 171–188.

Saner, Hans: Abwehr und Huldigung. Zu den Plänen einer wechselseitigen Kritik von Heidegger und Jaspers. In: ders.: *Einsamkeit und Kommunikation. Essays zur Geschichte des Denkens,* Basel 1994, 189–212.

Saner, Hans: Zum systematischen Ort der ethischen Reflexion im Denken von Karl Jaspers. In: *Jb. der Österreichischen Karl-Jaspers-Gesellschaft*, Bd. 12 (1999), 12–27.

Saner, Hans (Hg.): *Karl Jaspers. Was ist der Mensch? Philosophisches Denken für alle*, ausgewählt und mit einleitendem Kommentar von Hans Saner, München, Zürich 2000.

Saner, Hans: Überleben mit einer Jüdin in Deutschland. Karl und Gertrud Jaspers in der Zeit des Nationalsozialismus. In: ders.: *Erinnern und Vergessen. Essays zur Geschichte des Denkens*, Basel 2004, 97–130.

Saner, Hans: *Karl Jaspers*, Reinbek 2005.

Saner, Hans: Karl Jaspers on World History of Philosophy and World Philosophy. In: Kurt Salamun, Gregory J. Walters (eds.): *Karl Jaspers's Philosophy: Expositions and Interpretations*, Amherst, New York 2008, 89–106.

Sarin, Indu: Karl Jaspers and Asian Thought: Buddha and Nagarjuna. In: Kurt Salamun, Gregory J. Walters (eds.): *Karl Jaspers's Philosophy: Expositions and Interpretations*, Amherst, New York 2008, 291–312.

Sarin, Indu: *The Global Vision. Karl Jaspers*, Bern 2009.

Sartre, Jean Paul: *Das Sein und das Nichts. Versuch einer phänomenologischen Ontologie*, Hamburg 1962.

Scheler, Max: *Der Formalismus in der Ethik und die materiale Wertethik*, 4. Aufl. Bern 1954.

Schilpp, Paul A. (Hg.), *Karl Jaspers*, Stuttgart 1957.

Schmitt, Wolfram: Karl Jaspers als Psychiater und sein Einfluss auf die Psychiatrie. In: *Karl Jaspers in seiner Heidelberger Zeit*, hg. von Joachim-Felix Leonhard, Heidelberg 1983, 23–82.

Schneiders, Werner: *Karl Jaspers in der Kritik*, Bonn 1967.

Schüßler, Werner: Die bleibende Bedeutung des Mythos. Zum Mythosverständnis von Jaspers. In: *Jb. der Österreichischen Karl-Jaspers-Gesellschaft*, Jg. 29 (2016), 103–130.

Schwan, Alexander: *Politische Philosophie im Denken Heideggers*, 2., um einen Nachtrag 1988 erweiterte Auflage, Opladen 1989.

Sontheimer, Kurt: Einführung zur Neuausgabe, *Karl Jaspers, Wohin treibt die Bundesrepublik?* München, Zürich 1988, I–VII.

Stegmüller, Wolfgang: *Hauptströmungen der Gegenwartsphilosophie*, 3. erw. Aufl. Stuttgart 1965.

Stegmüller, Wolfgang: *Metaphysik, Skepsis, Wissenschaft*, 2. verb. Aufl. Berlin, Heidelberg, New York 1969.

Stelzer, Harald: Von Max Webers Gehäuse-Metapher zum Gehäuse-Begriff bei Karl Jaspers. In: *Studia Philosophica*, 67 (2008), 301–322.

Stelzer, Harald: Georg Simmel und Karl Jaspers. Gehäuse, Form und Leben. In: Oliver Immel, Harald Stelzer (Hg.): *Welt und Philosophie. Politik- kultur- und sozialphilosophische Beiträge zum Denken von Karl Jaspers*, Innsbruck, Wien 2011, S. 125–146.

Sternberger, Dolf: Jaspers und der Staat. In: Hans Saner (Hg.): *Karl Jaspers in der Diskussion*, München 1973, 418–423.

Tilliette, Xavier: *Karl Jaspers: Theorie de la verité, Metaphysique des chiffres, Foi philosophique*, Paris 1960.

Walters, Gregory J.: Jaspers's Philosophical Faith and Revelational Faith Today. Can the Two Faiths Meet in the Struggle for Human Liberation? In: Richard Wisser/Leonard H. Ehrlich (eds.): *Karl Jaspers. Philosopher among Philosophers*, Würzburg 1993, 217–227.

Weber, Alfred: Kulturgeschichte als Kultursoziologie. In: *Alfred Weber –Gesamtausgabe*, Bd. I, hg. von E. Demm, Marburg 1979.

Weber, Max: Wissenschaft als Beruf. In: ders.: *Gesammelte Aufsätze zur Wissenschaftslehre*, 3. erw. und verb. Aufl. Tübingen 1968a, 582–613.

Weber, Max: *Politik als Beruf*, Berlin 1968b.

Weidmann, Bernd: Der philosophische Glaube in der postsäkularen Gesellschaft. In: Anton Hügli, Dominic Kaegi, Bernd Weidmann (Hg.): *Existenz und Sinn. Karl Jaspers im Kontext, Festschrift für Reiner Wiehl*, Heidelberg 2009, 239–278.

Weidmann, Bernd: Gott als Person – Chiffre der Transzendenz oder mehr? In: *Jb. der Österreichischen Karl-Jaspers-Gesellschaft*, Jg. 26 (2013), 147–166.

Weidmann, Bernd: Einleitung des Herausgebers. In: ders. (Hg.): Karl Jaspers: Der philosophische Glaube angesichts der Offenbarung. In: *Karl Jaspers Gesamtausgabe*, Bd. I/13, Basel 2017, VII–LXXXIII.

Wiehl, Reiner: Jaspers' Bestimmung des Überpolitischen. In: Reiner Wiehl, Dominic Kaegi (Hg.): *Karl Jaspers – Philosophie und Politik*, Heidelberg 1999, 81–96.

Wisser, Richard/Leonard H. Ehrlich (eds.): *Karl Jaspers. Philosopher among Philosophers*, Würzburg 1993, 217–227.

Wittgenstein, Ludwig: *Tractatus logico-philosophicus*. In: ders.: *Werkausgabe, Bd. 1*, Frankfurt a. M. 1984.

Index

Made in the USA
Las Vegas, NV
11 May 2024

89824952R10090